Gang Prevention and Schools

The Ultimate Parent & Teacher Guide on How to Prevent Kids from Joining Gangs

By America's Leading Authority on Gang Prevention

RICHARD R. RAMOS

Published by Richard R. Ramos, Inc.

Printed in the United States of America

Library of Congress Control Number: 2008900266

Ramos, Richard R.

Gang Prevention and Schools – The Ultimate Parent & Teacher Guide on How to Prevent Kids from Joining Gangs / By Richard R. Ramos

ISBN - 13: 978-0-9814714-0-2

Warning – Disclaimer

The purpose of this book is to educate. The author or publisher does not guarantee that anyone following the techniques, suggestions, tips, ideas, or strategies will be successful in every circumstance. The author and publisher shall have neither liability nor responsibility to anyone with respect to any loss or damage caused, or alleged to be caused, directly or indirectly by the information contained in this book.

"PARENTS ON A MISSION"

A Leadership Movement for Gang Prevention

Parents on a Mission (POM) - a newly developed and specialized train the trainer curriculum tool for community leaders to develop parent leadership in homes, neighborhoods and schools as the best gang prevention strategy any community can invest in.

WHAT OTHERS ARE SAYING ABOUT RICHARD R. RAMOS

"I have a long history of working in corrections, and juvenile justice, and currently I am a Trustee on the Carpinteria Unified School District Board. After attending and listening to Richard's, "Parents on a Mission" presentation, I am 100% in agreement with his message to parents and communities on the best way to prevent children from joining gangs. His message is insightful, accurate, inspiring, but more than that, it is needed! If you want to make a difference in your school and community regarding gang prevention-intervention, then I wholeheartedly recommend Richard Ramos as the man you must hear!"

– Beverly Grant, Trustee Board of Education,
Carpinteria Unified School District

"I have been attending gang prevention-intervention seminars and presentation for 30 years. Richard's "Parents on a Mission" presentation is THE BEST I have ever heard or seen."

– Rich Medel, Director,
Boy's and Girls Club of Carpinteria

"We have had a lot of guest speakers address our students at one time or another. But I have never seen a speaker connect with and hold the attention of our kids like Richard did when he spoke to several of our schools with his unique style of delivering his anti-gang message. We need and want him back every year!"

– Dr. Brian Sarvis, Superintendent,
Santa Barbara School Districts

"My first encounter with Richard was at a forum on violence...he was the keynote speaker, and spoke on the topic of the angry heart. My heart was moved that day and forever changed after listening to his inspired message... he can help in a profound, unique and lasting way, if given the chance to simply speak."

– Honorable Denise De Bellefeuille,
Judge, Santa Barbara Municipal Court

"I have had the pleasure of watching the work of Richard Ramos for over a decade. When it comes to gang prevention & intervention strategies, Richard is a real results-oriented leader and innovator. He has helped hundreds of youth turn away from the gang lifestyle and I applaud his ongoing commitment to the young people of our nation."

– Charles Slosser, Ph.D President & CEO
Santa Barbara Foundation

This book is dedicated to my wife,
Christina…thank you honey for all of your
support, encouragement and patience in
allowing me the time and discipline behind
"closed doors" to accomplish my vision
and passion – I love you!

PREFACE

This work is a revised version of my first book, "Got Gangs?" This version is intended to be much more streamlined for parents and teachers for practical application on a daily basis. Although the reader will find some similar content from my first book, you will also notice new material with updated data to support my case for why I contend that building parent leadership in the home is the best gang prevention strategy any community can invest in. In addition, I have also created a "train the trainer" curriculum to go along with the material presented here for parents and teachers. For more information on how to obtain the manual please visit: www.RichardRRamos.com

Many practitioners confuse "intervention" with "prevention". For example, when a kid begins to act out, or commits their first misdemeanor or crime, practitioners begin to employ their strategy to "prevent" that youngster from joining a gang or continuing down the negative road he has started on. However, in my view, this is not "prevention", but rather, "intervention" to stop the youngster from committing further violations of the law. Of course this type of work is necessary, and effective in helping a youth turn from a lifestyle of committing more crimes and getting caught in the web of the Juvenile Justice system. I suggest that we need to take the issue a step further in working on root issues that will "prevent" a kid from ever going down the road of delinquency and joining a gang. This is my view of prevention and I believe many parents would prefer this rather than assuming, guessing, and hoping that their son or daughter never becomes a gang member in a gang neighborhood.

Guarantees? Well, what can anybody really guarantee in this life? The fact is, many good parents have done all the "right" things and have still suffered the heartaches of losing their kids to gangs and youth violence. Having said that, the fact also remains (according to the most recent research) that most kids are prevented from joining a gang, committing acts of violence, and never go down the road of juvenile delinquency. According to renowned gang research experts, Malcolm W. Klein and Cheryl L. Maxson:

> *"The best estimate of general U.S. youth gang prevalence is 5% ever-joined, 2% current gang members...Perhaps the strongest message in this research is that even with unrestricted definitions in high risk populations, most youth – 7 or 8 out of 10 – do not join gangs through adolescence."*
> *(Klein, Maxson, 2006. "Street Gang Patterns and Policies", Oxford University Press)*

Thus, in searching for answers to gang prevention, the question is not "Why do kids join gangs", but rather, "Why do most kids not join gangs?". This book focuses on the latter and advocates for community decision makers and practitioners to consider changing their focus from the problems gangs create to the problems that create gangs.

Richard R. Ramos

2008

TABLE OF CONTENTS

ABOUT THE AUTHOR

Richard R. Ramos is widely recognized throughout the U.S. as an expert on gang prevention and one of the most sought after Latino leaders and speakers on progressive and effective community leadership. With a twenty-eight year history of service, Richard brings a fresh leadership voice and vision that inspires and instructs individuals, families and communities on how to address today's real issues and develop a better quality of life for all. Ramos has written two books on gang prevention and intervention; *Gang Prevention and Schools – The Ultimate Parent & Teacher Guide on how to prevent kids from joining Gangs (2008) and Got Gangs? – Practical Guidance for Parents/Teachers on a Mission for Gang Prevention/Intervention (2006)*. He is also the author of *How to be a Great Latino Leader (2008)* and Co-founder of the Latino Coalition for Faith & Community Initiatives, a national nonprofit whose purpose is to strengthen and expand the capacity of nonprofits serving at-risk Latino youth and families. Under his leadership, the Latino Coalition is now working in more than twenty cities in seven states. Ramos' background has helped shape his unique blend of leadership qualities. Early in his career he served as a correctional officer in both state and federal prisons, a juvenile hall instructor and at-risk junior high and high school counselor, co-founding director of a gang intervention/prevention community coalition, director of a Latino youth and family teen center, Senior Pastor for sixteen years, and founding director of the Interfaith Initiative of Santa Barbara County. For his work in the field of human rights and interfaith understanding, he has received numerous accolades and awards:

- January 2007 recognized by President Bush for community leadership and service
- February 2007 U.S. Congressional recognition for outstanding and invaluable contribution to US communities.
- February 2007 California State Assembly recognition for community service
- March 2005 recognized as a national interfaith leader through his induction into the Morehouse Colleges Martin Luther King, Jr. International Chapels Board of Preachers, Sponsors and Collegium of Scholars an international body of leaders recognized for their efforts in reconciliation to people of all faiths and their support of diverse "communities of hope."
- November 2003 nominated for the Baha'i Human Rights Award, and received "honorable mention" for exemplary services to the community.
- August 2003 received award from the United Religious Initiative and Parliament of the World's Religions in recognition and honor of service to promoting interfaith understanding.
- 1996 received Congressional recognition for "outstanding and invaluable contribution to the community."
- 1995 honored as "community advocate of the year" by the Hispanic Business Council of the Chamber of Commerce of Santa Barbara
- In 1994 voted by Santa Barbara High School District students as one of the most influential leaders in the community.

INTRODUCTION

The First Family is not in the White House,
it's in Your House

As American citizens we have been raised with the concept that the "First Family" refers to the family of the President of the United States, which resides in Washington D.C. in what we refer to as the "White House". This is an important honor we give the presiding President and his family as we recognize their leadership, position of authority and convey respect for their family. Thus, when I say, "the First Family is not in the White House, it's in your house", it is in no way intended to disrespect or take anything away from the honor of the office of our President. Rather, it is an attempt on my part to use this well known metaphor to catch the attention of parents and drive home a message about the importance of their role in raising their kids as the best means of preventing them from joining gangs.

I am reminded of a conversation I had one day as I was attending the birthday party of one of my church members' children. The grandfather of the child was there and as we were sitting together, we had the following exchange:

"Richard, I want to ask you a question. A lot of kids in this community listen to you and with all the problems we are having with gangs and violence and these kinds of kids, why don't you get them all together and talk to them?" I replied, *"Well that would certainly be helpful and I have and will continue to do that. But, I don't think that is really the best way to handle this situation".* He looked at me somewhat puzzled and said, *"What do you mean?" I replied, "Well, since you are a gardener by profession; let me put it to you in a way that I know you will understand. If you walked by your neighbors garden and saw that the flowers were all wilted, dry and dying, who would you rather talk to, the flowers or the gardener?"* With that a smile broke out on his face and in Spanish he agreed and said that I made a good point to which he had not previously considered.I explained to him that our children were like the flowers in our garden and the parents were like the gardeners, and if we really wanted to make the best and most effective prevention impact, it would be the work done with "gardeners", more than just the "flowers". Thus, the first hand experience I have gained throughout my 25 plus years of working with gang members and at-risk Latino youth & families has lead me to the conclusion that parent-child relationships are the key to prevention. This may seem too simple and obvious, but as I continue to examine and study these problems and talk with those involved in gangs or considered "at-risk" for joining a gang, it usually comes right down to the parent-child relationship, or lack thereof, that is at the root of these problems.

I realize this point of view puts a lot of pressure on parents and lays much of the carcass of blame at their feet. Although I do not believe the parents are always to blame for every child who goes astray, I do however think that if we parents are willing to take part of the credit for the success of our children, we ought to be just as willing to accept part of the blame when our children fail. This does not mean that the parent is a bad person, negligent, or abusive. But what I have found is many parents have simply never really learned many of the things I discuss in this book. Those who have learned these principles and practice them, in most cases, have healthy relationships with their kids who are leading productive lives. These parents probably learned how to have a healthy relationship with their kids from their parents, or whoever was the principle person who raised them as children. Yet, all too often, many of us lacked parents who exemplified healthy human relationships and thus we end up using the age old philosophy of child rearing; *"If it was good enough for me, its good enough for you"*. In order to examine if this age old philosophy is a correct view to practice in raising our children, we have to first look within ourselves and be honest about what the practices of our parents produced in our own emotional healthiness. Next, if we already have children, we must look at what these "inherited" child rearing practices are producing in our own children and their relationships with their siblings, relatives, teachers, friends and authority figures of which parents are the most important.

In working with the problem of gangs, the focus is usually on "what they are doing", rather than on "what they are missing" that other "normal" kids, who live in the same neighborhoods, go to the same schools and play in the same playgrounds, seem to have that gang members don't have. As we have come to learn, gangs are nothing more than substitutes for parents and family life that all human beings desire to be a part of. All of us have the same need to be accepted as we are, loved for who we are, and given attention, dignity, respect, and self-worth. We all have a need for the emotional, intellectual, social and spiritual potential. I suggest it is this fundamental understanding that is often overlooked when seeking solutions for children and teens that have gone astray. Contrary to popular belief, kids want to respect their parents and live in a healthy, happy relationship with them. But almost all of the gang members I have talked with did not have it and were really broken hearted about it. It became the hole in their hearts that they have tried to fill with gangs, drugs, alcohol, sex and other negative stuff that just does not fill that hole, no matter how hard and long they have tried to fill it with these other things. I would even go so far as to say that even "good" kids who are successful in sports, academics, or other socially acceptable activities, yet don't have a healthy, happy relationship with their parents, also have that same hole or emptiness of heart, and nothing, not even "success", can fill it like the unconditional love and acceptance of a parent.

Thus, as we continue to search for answers to a number of issues regarding youth that are being heavily influenced by gangs, I suggest that one of the most important messages we can support is encouraging parent leadership in the home. Parent leadership simply means to consistently make every possible effort to invest our time, talents and money into our own personal growth and relationships in our own home first and thereby communicate to our children that they are the number one priority in our lives, which I contend is the key tool of preventing kids from joining gangs. In addition to the influence of parents, teachers are in the second most powerful position of influence and shaping the self-image of children. I will discuss the role of teachers in part III of the book.

A number of years ago I was asked by a community group organizing a coalition to stop gang violence in South Santa Barbara County, to come and speak at a community forum on the causes of acts of violence by youth. As we all know, the gang lifestyle, among other things, includes acts of violence. In fact, the initiation for gang membership is an act of violence referred to as "jumped in", which is a short period of time (usually lasting a minute or two, or more in some cases) where a number of members of the gang beat up on the new member as a way of showing their toughness and desire to be a part of the gang. That in itself is bad enough, but as we know, the violence does not stop there. Thus, as I prepared for my talk, I began to think deeply and draw upon all the knowledge and insight I had gained from listening to so many gang members tell me their story and their reasons for doing the things they were doing.. What I eventually came up with to share that day, has become a foundational theme I speak on every chance I get in my desire to help families and communities address the root issues of gangs and youth violence. The following is the thought I shared that day:

> *"Acts of violence are caused by an angry heart and an angry heart is produced by unresolved injustices (real or perceived) that young people experienced as victims usually in their own homes."*

These "unresolved injustices" can range from sexual, physical, verbal and emotional abuse suffered from any number of family members in the privacy of the home. My goal in writing to parents (and those who work with parents) is to inspire us to take a moment to look inside our own hearts and be honest about any injustices we may have been a part of, and then provide instruction on how to turn our hearts towards our children, and find the strength to deal with these unresolved issues that our children may have been carrying in their hearts for years. I know this is not easy and can be very uncomfortable, but if we can find the courage or professional help to take this loving action, I know it will make a great difference in preventing kids from joining gangs, and/or successfully intervening to cause our kids already in a gang to quit and leave the gang more than any other single factor! I know this to be true because I have done it with my own kids and so many other youth have told me it is true, over and over again in juvenile hall cells, prison cells, letters, school classrooms, counseling sessions, and various other public and private settings. Thus, this book is specifically written for parents and teachers who have a burden for kids at-risk for joining gangs or already in a gang and wondering what to do and where to go for help. With you in mind, I have been inspired to write with the intention of providing encouragement, guidance and hope that can cause heart revelation, heart revolution and home reconciliation of the peace, harmony and love all families were intended to know.

Sincerely,
Richard R. Ramos

PART II

GANG PREVENTION

CHAPTER 1

Why kids join Gangs

*"Hey I am a 14 year old girl and I am in the 8th grade. I have a lot of friends that are in gangs. Well my homegirl said then why don't I join her barrio so should I? Cause life at home is f***ed up big time. So I think if I join they will treat me like family so what should I do? ISN'T THERE ANYTHING GOOD ABOUT BEING IN A GANG?"*

"Hi I'm 11 and I was thinking about joining a gang. That's because my mom and dad aren't together. I live with my mom and my mom has a boyfriend who hates me. I never get to see my dad because he's always in jail and I'm moving out of my mom's house as soon as I can but the only skills I have are fighting and gun shooting what should I do?"

*"Hi my name is Sara and I'm 15 years old. I've been wanting to join a gang for the longest time because I have a lot of problems at home. The thing is that I don't get along with my parents or brothers because my mom treats me like a f****ing dog or if I was some kind of slut, but I'm not. For some reason my parents have always treated me different like if I was some kind of mistake in their lives and I have a lot of friends in gangs and they're always happy and treat each other all nice and they*

protect each other and since my parents don't give a damn about me I think I should join it. I don't care what I have to do to get in as long as someone loves and takes care of me for the first time. I don't care. What do you think I should do?"

(Quotes taken from: www.gangsandkids.com)

"Why do kids join gangs?" - Over the years this is probably one of, if not *thee most,* asked question I have received from parents, educators, and other concerned adults. The solution to preventing kids from joining gangs can seem complex and overwhelming, especially to those of us who have been on the front lines and are witnessing the growing numbers of elementary and junior high school students that are acting out violently or joining gangs. However, although the solution may be somewhat complex, it does not mean that the cause of these problems is always equally complex. In my mind, the better question to ask is, *"Why is it that most kids don't join gangs?"* - I suggest this approach because this gives us the answer to the prevention question. The fact is, the answer to preventing kids from joining gangs has been right under our nose all along. We have missed the obvious because oftentimes our tendency is to focus on the negative instead of the positive when it comes to solving problems.

While I don't want to oversimplify why kids join gangs, what I have found in most cases is that the root of this problem lies in the parent child relationship, or non- relationship. And thus it follows that the answer to prevention lies in the same place. Consider this, no neighborhood or school, where gangs are known to exist, can claim that "most of the kids" in the neighborhood or school are in a gang. The plain truth is most are not and I contend that the reason for this is the home they are raised in. I came to this conclusion after I conducted an informal survey among the many gang members, and their families that I have worked with over the past 25 plus years. I could see as they began to speak from their hearts so many things were happening at once. I could see relief to be who they really were, burdens were lifted as the words they spoke revealed hurt they had been carrying for years, and their eyes were opened in a new way to themselves. Much of this took place in group settings among their fellow gang members in my office, their homes, at school, or in a park. It was an incredible time of learning, bonding, and growing for all of us. It is very rewarding today, years later, to run into them as young adults throughout the community with their children. We laugh and joke about all the times they used to visit my office for being in trouble.

However, the point I want to focus on is the significance of the consistent response I received as I continually asked them "why" they acted in such destructive, defiant, and violent ways.

The number one response I heard was that they were unhappy at home.

Not all of them said it exactly in those words, but it became more and more evident that ultimately, one of the root causes of their bad choices in behavior had something to do with unhealthy and disrespectful relationships with their parents and/or guardians. Again, I want to emphasize, this is not to suggest that their parents/guardians were bad people or that parents are always to blame for every kid who joins a gang or goes astray in one manner or another. But neither should we ignore the significance of the role parents play in the life of their children as stated by these gang members. Let me also note that most of the time their tone in talking about this was not one of anger as much as one of sadness. This response was consistent from many different gang members (boys and girls), of different ages, and different sides of town over a period of several years that I was asking this question. Thus, I began communicating with parents the crucial importance of giving priority to the proper and consistent nurture to their kids as a normal part of their daily lives and never to take for granted how children value and need their time, attention, approval, encouragement and unconditional love. While I know it is true that there are some kids who come from "healthy homes" that join gangs, this clearly is the exception and not the rule. Here is one young girl's story:

> *Growing up...My mom was never around, from what I understand she left us when I was a baby, but my dad never talks about it. I lived with my dad moving from town to town, never knowing where we were going to settle at. Although I lived with my dad I never saw much of him, and that just led to my conclusion that he didn't care about me.*
>
> *A few years later I was able to see my mom again. She had turned into a crack addict, so she didn't have that good of an influence over me. At times I would stay the weekend with my mom at her apartment, only to wake up in the middle of the night scared and alone. Physically my dad never beat me, but verbally it was like torture. It was like walking on egg shells around him, if I so much as*

breathed the wrong way around him he would get in my face and scream at me until I broke down and cried. He would leave me alone for a while, just long enough for me to dry my tears, and then he would come back in for another round. It was like a never ending cycle, and I was so sick of the repetition that I just wanted to end it for myself. I honestly didn't want to live anymore. By the age of 12, I had attempted suicide a numerous amount of times.

By the age of 13 I started hanging around gangs. First I hung out with a bunch of older guys from the 18th St. gang, until I was raped by a supposed homeboy. I couldn't believe someone I had trusted would take away my virginity like that. But I figured if it was no longer special why not just give it up more. Once I was in 8th grade I thought I had met my best friend. We always hung out together. He was the one who introduced me to the rest of the surenos from 13. I started hanging out with them everyday, wanting so badly to fit in with them. On Halloween I thought I had finally figured out where I belonged when I got jumped into their gang. Being the first and only girl I had to get my ass kicked by three guys at once. These vatos were huge! I threw up nothing but blood for like 2 days, I was so sore. I couldn't even move without cringing in pain. To prove myself I got mi tres puntos, or my three dots. It was supposed to be a symbol of my crazy life, but it is now a symbol of shame for me. Before I would dress from head to toe in blue, throw trece to anyone and everyone, and I was so proud of my 3 dots. They were like my babies, now it just embarrasses me.

Pretty soon I was sneaking my dad's tequila bottles, adding water so he wouldn't notice how much I took. I would skip school on a daily basis just to go get high. Soon I was introduced to pills. I was hooked from the start. It wasn't until I almost overdosed that I realized the harm they were doing to my body. All my good grades turned to F's, I got dropped from almost all my classes because of poor attendance, and I was no longer my daddy's little girl. Instead of being his pride and joy I just embarrassed him. I felt like I had truly hit my rock bottom.

After getting kicked out of my house I finally listened to my cousin and went to church with her. I did not expect to like it; I just thought it would be a good way to meet hot guys who would treat me good. From the moment I walked in and saw the hugs everyone gave my cousin, or the way that everyone reached out to each other I knew why my life had felt so empty. I needed love like this, and never before did I ever want anything as bad as I wanted that right then. Sure getting high would take away my pain and leave me happy, but that is only until I would come down. Then my life would be just as empty as it was before. From the moment that the pastor had started his sermon I felt like it was directed at me. When he made his Altar call I was one of the first people down there on my knees. I let years of pain, anger, and resentment drip out of me as my tears fell onto the Altar. I felt so much better.

If I would have known that being saved would feel this good I would have done it years ago. I can't go back and change yesterday, but I can look forward tomorrow. It is such a relief to know that I do not have to face it alone anymore, now I have the Lord on my side. I wasted way too many years being lost.

Mariposa

Although this young girl, Mariposa, found refuge in church, my point in sharing her story is the references she makes about the kind of relationship she had with her parents and the effect it had on some of her choices. However, the positive lesson we can learn from this negative story as parents is the understanding of how much influence we have on the hearts of our children and to use that to plant good, positive and loving "seeds" in the hearts of our children, especially during their young formative years. The abandonment Mariposa felt from her mother and the verbal abuse she received from her father can be replaced by our investment of time with our kids and listening to them, rather than always speaking at them. Although this may seem a bit intimidating, to know how our every action affects our children, in my view as a parent, it gives me a lot of hope to know that I am, or at least can be, the chief architect of my child's early development. It gives me hope to know that the chief influence of my children is under my control and care, rather than some strange or uncontrollable force "out there". It gives me hope to know that my presence, ears, eyes and words count more to my children than anyone else, and it inspires me to want to be a better parent, knowing the pressure my children are facing in society on the school campus and through today's music, media and movies. This understanding caused me to realize how much hope and empowerment I could give worried parents once they realized that a big part of the solution to their problem was not "out there" somewhere, but rather, right in their own home, indeed, right in their own hearts!

As I began to teach this, I noticed the hope it gave parents. I shared with them the things I was hearing from teenagers and developed practical principles to help build their parenting skills. I emphasized the importance of parents accepting the challenge to look within themselves first as a fundamental principle of finding solutions to the behavior problems they had with their children. I challenged them to examine their own assumptions and levels of emotional maturity as a possible cause of the problem. I asked them to re-examine their priorities of where they had been investing their time. After teaching these principles over two year's time, we began to see results in the healing and reconciliation of many broken and wounded hearts in parents, their children and many of the young gang members attending our services. Here is one example of a young man I am very proud of:

> *My name is Phillip Rendon and I am 26 years old (2002). I am currently employed at CompuWave of Ventura and serve as manager of the CompuWave Customer Care Center. My wife and I live in Oxnard, Ca with our four children, Marie, Briana, Phillip Jr. and Isaiah.*
>
> *I was born in Santa Barbara, Ca in 1976. I spent most of my child hood moving between Santa Barbara, Oxnard and San Bernardino County. For as long as I could remember, I had been around gang members in one way or another. My biological father was a gang member that*

has been in prison since 1978. My mother was also a well-known Santa Barbara gang member in her youth. My first real influence in the gang life style was with my older cousin Brad Fowler, who has since passed away.

My mother and stepfather raised us the way that seemed normal to them at the time. Growing up as a young man it was not uncommon to see physical, emotional, alcohol and drug abuse. All of these elements produced the bitter and angry young man I would become. Violence was the normal means of releasing all of my frustration and became a common occurrence for me. I was naturally drawn to the gang life style. At the age of about 12, I started to emulate all that I saw in my cousin and his friends. Under my parent's nose, I had adopted the gang clothing and attitude. I had the attitude that all authority figures were against me, and I rebelled every chance that I had. This led to many problems in school and at home.

When I turned 15, I had already been sent to San Bernardino County Juvenal hall and had been kicked out of school for my violent behavior. My mother finally sent me to live with my aunt in Santa Barbara, because she could no longer control me. From the first day that I arrived in Santa Barbara, I had it in my mind to officially join the East Side gang that many members of my family belonged to. I started out by being overly aggressive in violent acts against rival gang members. In 1992 I took part in my full initiation in to the East Side "Krazies" gang in Santa Barbara. The initiation consisted of being beaten by fellow gang members for 60 seconds.

In my eyes I had arrived. Becoming an official member of my gang was all that I had ever-wanted to do. The gang became my family. My parents had, in my eyes, treated me wrong, but now I belonged to a group that made me feel important. There were many times that my fellow gang members had put their own lives on the line for me and I would do the same for them. Finally I was happy! I felt as if I was on the top of the world. I had seen people shot, stabbed and beaten nearly to death. None of these things mattered to any of us. The gang was all that we knew or cared to know.

Around that time Richard Ramos started a youth group in the heart of our neighborhood. I didn't take any of this seriously at first. There would often be 20 to 35 young people packed into this small 3 bedroom home. It became the talk of the neighborhood. I would go because everyone else was there, but stayed outside. We would even make fun of anyone that started to outwardly show interest.

One Wednesday night, I was out with some friends drinking and making our rounds, around the East Side. Mr. Ramos drove up and asked if I wanted to go eat. We made small talk for a few brief moments and then I agreed to go. I was under the impression that we were going to a restaurant, but we eventually drove up to his house.

His wife and children all seemed so laid back to me. As we all sat down to eat we bowed our heads and gave thanks for the food. Mr. Ramos went around the table and asked all of his children how their days had went. They all seemed to be so happy to be at the table together. You could tell that there was genuine love in this family and I was impressed. That night just happened to be a church night and I decide to go with them to service. During the service all I could do was think about my family. I could remember a time that things weren't so bad at home. We used to pray together and it seemed like we loved each other. At that moment my heart was filled with love for my parents and I wished that they were there with me.

Toward the end of the service...all of the weights that life had placed on my shoulders seemed to leave. For the first time in years I broke down and cried. I didn't care who was around, because I genuinely felt free from all of the anger and bitterness. From that night on I was never the same. I never went back to the gang life style. I disassociated myself altogether from my gang.

I would later meet my wife Josie at church. She too was a gang member and had been invited to church by a teacher. Josie was also transformed on her first visit to the church. She grew up in an abusive household as well and had been heavily involved in drugs in addition to the gang.

Since that night in 1992, I was never the same. We are blessed to be raising children that will not grow up in the gang and drug environment. Our children have an advantage in life that neither Josie nor I had growing up. My wife and I are training to work with disadvantaged youth and families, hoping to give back a portion of what we have received.

We are dedicated to the family and believe that by teaching others to put family first, we can save young people and parents from the mistakes that we made. In doing so we hope to help our community by strengthening the very fabric that makes up the community, which is the family.

Sincerely,
Phillip J. Rendon

It has been five years since Phillip first wrote his story and today he continues on as strong as ever to not only build his own family, but reaching out to his community to touch and turn around the lives of other gang members.

I realize that there are other factors that cause kids to join gangs apart from their relationship with their parents, peer pressure being one of them. When I considered the mass number of parents who were searching for concrete answers and solutions, I knew it was important to focus on the things they could control. Thus, my purpose is to urge parents, police, probation officers, principals of schools, politicians, pastors and other concerned community leaders that the best prevention strategy we can focus on to stop kids from desiring to join gangs is the parent-child relationship.

CHAPTER 2

Gang Suppression is not Prevention

"In short, gang proliferation has changed important aspects of our society and seldom in desirable ways. Thus the extent to which responses are based on inappropriate, conventional wisdom versus accumulated fact-based understandings takes on special importance."
– Malcolm Klein

In 2006, according the Department of Justice, across the country there are approximately 24-31,000 gangs and gang membership nationwide is estimated at around 760,000. Latino youth and families, as the largest and fastest growing minority population in the U.S., are at the greatest risk of gang involvement. According to the most recent National Youth Gang Survey (2006), nearly half (49 percent) of all gang members are Hispanic/Latino, 34 percent are African American/black, 10 percent are Caucasian/white, 6 percent are Asian, and the remainder are of some other race/ethnicity. Although crime rates have been falling for more than 10 years, gang violence is said to be increasing as a proportion of overall violent crime and receiving national attention. Newsweek's March 28, 2005 issue featured an article entitled "The Most Dangerous Gang in America," a description of the Mara Salvatrucha—or MS-13—a growing and violent force claiming 10,000 members from coast to coast. In a follow-up article in the Los Angeles Times (May 15, 2005 front page story), it was stated that MS-13 has between 30,000 to 50,000 members across half a dozen countries and is the cause of the FBI forming its first nation wide task force targeting a single street gang. Although these statistics have been recently challenged (see www.justicepolicy.org – New report debunks gang crime myths), youth violence is a problem and our nation's communities are crying out for solutions. However, as we seek to provide solutions, we must also assess the effectiveness of our past efforts that have relied heavily on law enforcement at the local level. Clearly, this strategy has failed and we cannot continue to invest our resources in failed methods, yet I fear that is exactly what decision makers continue to do in spite of the data that is screaming for new solutions to gang prevention and intervention.

As of this writing, once again, the city of Los Angeles has "declared war" on gangs, singling them out as the "enemy". I say "again" because this tactic and concentration on L.A. gangs had been tried before by a former L.A.P.D. Chief, Daryl Gates, as well as by the current Chief of Police and city attorney, and by their own admission, have not been successful.

According to the Advancement Project (January 2007–www.advanceproj.com), a study of gang violence in Los Angeles County, commissioned by the L.A. City Council:

> *"After a quarter century of a multi-billion dollar war on gangs, there are six times as many gangs and at least double the number of gang members in the region. Suppression alone... cannot solve this problem. Law*

enforcement officials now agree that they cannot arrest their way out of violence crisis and that their crime suppression efforts must be linked to competent prevention, intervention, and community-stabilizing investment strategies...In sum, despite decades of research into gangs and violence, there is no single, definitive formula for success in reducing either. Even federal authorities who have invested heavily into gang suppression strategies note, 'Although thousands of programs have been implemented...the ongoing difficulties with youth gangs make one lesson very clear: there are no quick fixes or easy solutions for the problems that youth gangs create or the problems that create youth gangs.' And leading gang researcher Malcolm Klein recently noted that the quest for how to end gang activity and violence remains largely unanswered."

In spite of these findings, the U.S. Congress continues to take the suppression approach. It is troubling to me that decision makers continue to listen to the rhetoric for more law enforcement suppression and the call to increase our judicial power to prosecute more juveniles as adults. In another recent report, *Ganging Up on Communities, putting Gang Crime in Context, July 2005,* released by the Justice Policy Institute (www.justicepolicy.org), stated the following:

Although crime has been decreasing in the United States for the past twelve years, many people fear that violent crime, especially gang-related crime, is rising...Currently, public opinion is swayed by sensationalized stories from media and lawmakers who say that gang-related crime is a "national crisis," requiring new federal and state legislation, mandatory minimums, and new powers to arrest, detain, imprison, and deport young people... The "Gang Prevention and Effective Deterrence Act of 2005" (S. 155) is winding its way through the Senate, and would create new gang offenses, enhance existing penalties, lower the number of people defined as a gang from five to three, and transfer more youth to adult courts and prisons. The Senate bill comes after the passage of a House bill, the "Gang Deterrence and Community Protection Act of 2005" (H.R. 1279), which calls for new mandatory minimums for gang-related offenses, and an expansion of the death penalty. The reach of the gang crisis is portrayed as broad and omnipresent, said to connect to everything from drug trafficking, to immigration, to terrorism. In June, Representative J. Randy Forbes (R-VA) introduced the "Alien Gang Removal Act" (H.R. 2933), a bill that authorizes the Department of Homeland Security (DHS) to deport groups, and associations that are designated as "criminal street gangs." These bills were introduced to reduce gang crime, yet they rely almost exclusively on approaches that have been shown to be the most expensive and least effective ways to respond to crime. Responding to provisions to transfer youth to adult prison, Robert Shepherd, Professor of Law at the University of Richmond and former Virginia prosecutor, says: "this bill flies in the face of what works with young

> *people ...the evidence shows that trying young people as adults exacerbates rather than lessens crime." Shepherd suggests that "rather than federalizing crime with policies that will not solve the problem, we should provide federal resources and support for state intervention and prevention programs."*

The point is, increased law enforcement has been tried repeatedly and it is time to invest our resources in a different approach. Again, that is not to say that law enforcement is not needed at all, or that they do not have an important and appreciated role to play in dealing with this problem. I am simply suggesting that we give more attention to the data which does not support the "war on gangs-suppression" approach as the best or most effective way of prevention of gang activity.

CHAPTER 3

Gang members are not the enemy

"Fostering a national culture of fear
concerning gangs only diverts our attention
from the real problem and real solutions."

– Ganging up on Communities Study,
Justice Policy Institute

Every gang member is a human being first with the same human needs that we all have. I believe it is this fundamental approach that has allowed me the success in turning many of these young hearts away from the gang lifestyle. This is not to say we should ignore the wrong things they do, especially acts of violence and crime. However, there is a reason for violent behavior and when those reasons are effectively addressed and understood; human hearts change and the results are revolutionary.

The school, principal, teacher, policeman, or community member should not view every gang member as "the enemy." This kind of perception causes a posture of offensiveness, defensiveness and pre-judgment that is keenly felt by a gang member at home, on the street or in a classroom. After all, contrary to popular opinion, not every gang member commits acts of violence or causes problems in the community. Troublemakers and those who act violently come from many different sectors and social classes of society and come in every size, shape, gender and race and I believe that our society is very tired of a double standard of justice. Our generation has grown up watching too many seemingly social "V.I.P.'s", who are guilty of one crime or another, but get off with the proverbial "hand slap." Justice must be equally applied and that is not always easy to do when one side is seen as the "good guy" and the other as "the enemy." It is easier to justify illegal, inappropriate, and antagonistic behavior when it is perceived as being done by "the good guys". For example, consider the comment of one student gang member:

> *"One teacher grabbed me by the hair and yelled at me...I pushed her and she fell on the floor and injured one of her fingers. I was suspended for six months"*

In the above case, the teacher received no reprimand, the student dropped out of school. The point is not to blame the school or teacher for the decision of this gang member. That is his/her responsibility. But, the double standard of applying the rules, one set for students, and another set for teachers, police and other authority figures, is unfortunately all too common. Our efforts should be focused on the real enemies which, in my opinion, are what tear at the root and destroy the foundation of our nation which is fast becoming an endangered species, and that is the American family. **In other words, we should not focus so much of our time and resources on the problems that gangs create as much as on the problems that create gangs.**

At this juncture let me take a moment to acknowledge that, on the other hand, there does seem to be a gang "evolution" in the sophistication of some of the prison and street gangs that warrant a stepped up law enforcement focus. This is not a contradiction to what I have been saying, but an important distinction that needs to be understood as we look for solutions to gangs and youth violence.

Being in a gang or associated with a gang never seemed to be such a serious matter as it has become over the past several years. A street gang was simply a bunch of neighborhood youth that formed a loose and vaguely organized group that basically joined together to party, hang out and back each other up when it came to fighting with rival gangs. Other than that, things were kept pretty simple. Although there were times where crimes like stealing or burglary were committed either out of need or mischievousness, I never considered a street gang in the same way as the "Mafia" or other sophisticated organized crime groups.

"First and foremost, we need to recognize that gang members spend much more time hangin' than bangin'"
– Malcolm Klein

However, times have changed and some prison and street gangs are now considered to have evolved to a point of sophistication that warrants increased law enforcement systems and strategies from the highest levels of our government. I am not in a position to comment as to whether or not this is justified, but only want to recognize that there are some prison and street gangs that seem to operate at a different level than the kind of gangs and gang members that I have been speaking about.

In a recent book on the Mexican Mafia, the author states:

The EME/street gang enterprise may not be as well organized as La Cosa Nostra, but it doesn't mean it's

thoroughly disorganized. Importing and distributing drugs, collecting proceeds, keeping out competitors, taxing the dealers and funneling the money into prisons requires at least a functional level of organization...to deny a functioning organization is to deny reality...Street gangsters are often the puppets of the big homies locked up in prison. The proof is overwhelming and plays itself out on almost a daily basis in almost every neighborhood in Southern California."
(Rafael, Tony. 2007. The Mexican Mafia, Encounter Books, New York & London)

What I am advocating for in this book is more for the younger and less sophisticated gangs and gang members that are common in our local neighborhoods, schools and those that still live at home or have consistent connection with their parents and extended families. Thus, while I understand there exists so called sophisticated national and international gangs, such as Surenos – 13, Mara Salvatrucha – 13, 18th Street Gang, Latin Kings, Mexican Mafia, Asian Boyz and the Jamaican Posse, to name a few, we should not make the mistake of classifying all gangs and gang members in this category and lump all gangs and all gang members under the same laws, enforcement strategies and attitudes. Moreover, even the hardest of these gangs and gang members are not beyond the reach of the arm of compassion. The untold story in this arena is the effectiveness of the faith community in reaching out and transforming the lives of literally tens of thousands of hard core gang members (as most police and gang practitioners know) during the same time in which gangs have grown over the past forty years. Our national media refuses to tell this story and usually only depicts the negative, harsh and ugly reality of violence perpetrated by these gangs, but as I stated earlier, gang members are human beings before they are anything else, and they have the same human needs that we all have and given the right circumstances and opportunity, any gang member can change at anytime and should not be looked on as the enemy.

"Are you still in a gang or did you change and get out?
If not why? If so how and what made you change?"
– Andrea

"No, I'm not in a gang anymore. I decided to change my life when I noticed that my homies were only there for me when it was convenient and not when I was in trouble or locked up. Only my family has always been by my side. If one would stop and consider things, one would come to realize that those who claim to be closest to you will be the ones who'll betray you whether it be by going out with your partner or simply by taking possessions, etc. If there's someone you can count on, it's family."
– Jesse (www.gangsandkids.com)

CHAPTER 4

Parents on a Mission – the key to Prevention

"My parents were very involved in the civil rights movement of the late 60s and early 70s and were committed members of a local militant group known as the "Brown Berets". During this time, (the early 70s) there was a lot of partying around me and at the age of nine years old, I remember being aware of things that other children my age were not aware of. I chose to become an angry child and by the time I was eleven years old I had become a racist child. I often got into fights with children of other ethnicities and purposely sought to separate my fellow Mexican American class mates from Anglo children. In the sixth grade, I was expelled from school for bringing marijuana on campus. I was expelled again in the 8th grade for hospitalizing a classmate in a fight. I started smoking marijuana everyday at the age of fourteen and became a gang member that same year (1981). Even though my family objected to my life style and had tried many times to intervene in my destructive behavior, I continued abusing alcohol and cocaine almost every day and occasionally I injected heroin"

- Pastor Ron Urzua, Oxnard, CA, reflecting on the influence of his upbringing

It makes me happy to hear much more talk today about the importance of the family and parents as the key to gang prevention. Many communities are now using various forms of parenting classes as a means to help build better parent-child relationships. The California legislature recently passed a law that allows the court to mandate parents of gang members to enroll in parenting classes and programs (California Welfare & Institution Code § 727.7). I began advocating this strategy back in the early nineties through my "parents on a mission" classes I taught every week in my church. Since that time I have come to realize a very important and distinct difference between "parent classes" and "parent leadership" that is an important point to understand.

I suggest the notion of classes does not go far enough to impress upon parents their need for personal growth and development of themselves first, before they are qualified to lead their children in the same. What usually happens is that parents end up making demands on their children to live a standard they are not willing to live themselves. This causes much frustration for kids as they grow older and resist the old, "do as I say, not as I do" message from their parents. This is true in many situations when people in positions of authority are gaining head knowledge from classes they take, but don't see the knowledge as something they need to apply to their personal lives first, before they can lead others to do the same. This double standard is always surrounded by controversy, confusion, criticism and broken relationships.

Parents on a Mission (POM) are parents who provide leadership in the home. POM is an inside-out approach to personal growth and influence. POM emphasizes that leadership is a matter of character, as well as, a matter of skill. It is a matter of earning the trust of those we want to follow us, namely our children. In general, parent classes attempt to increase competency without laying the foundation of character. While the inside-out leadership approach is challenging for parents as it calls them to personal accountability, to ignore this principle causes even more challenges for parents in the long run and therefore is vital to the POM training.

Most parents struggling with their kids just want to know how to fix their kids, not themselves. They usually do not see themselves as part of the problems they are having with their children anymore than a boss at work sees him/herself as part of the problem with a less than enthusiastic and loyal staff. Thus, they send their staff off to trainings, classes and seminars on the newest fad of "team building" only to find that nothing changes in the work place and more money is spent on hiring and training new employees because of the high turn over rate year after year. This can cause an employer to become frustrated and cynical about investing time and money in "training". However, the training classes may not be the problem, but rather the lack of buy in by the boss to personally lead their staff and demonstrate the type of character and competence desired and expected in the work place. The same can happen with parents after attending parent classes. If they don't see any change in their children they can become frustrated and drop out of the classes. What they are missing is the understanding that they need to take the lead and "be the change" they wish to see in their children and thereby creating the environment their children can respond to. For this reason, I continue to advocate for more emphasis on the need for more parent mentors. We are so used to hearing about the need for youth mentors, but we also need parent mentors and maybe even more so (for more information to become certified to be a POM trainer visit: www.RichardRRamos.com).

Thus, when I speak about "Parents on a Mission" (POM) as the answer to gang prevention, I am speaking about parent leadership in the home demonstrated by their own dedication to being a role model of the principles of personal growth and character development they want for their children. When parents provide a model of healthy and mature growth they provide children with the motivation for their own healthy, happy growth and maturity!

Foundations for Parental Leadership

1. Know yourself to grow yourself:

It took me years to understand this basic principle of success and leadership. I heard about it and read about it, but did not really understand it until I came to different places of failure, frustration and the challenges of raising my own family. I distinctly remember the emotions going on inside of me when my children were expressing their own emotions through crying, whining or verbally complaining as they grew older. Soon I began to question and ask myself why I was feeling the way I felt and why was I getting angry, impatient and intolerant of kids simply being kids? How was it that their moods were controlling mine? Eventually through study and self reflection I came to understand, "know thyself", and if my kids were going to be happy, I needed to be happy within myself. I realized that I could not emotionally be there for my kids until I satisfied my own emotional needs and grew out of trumping their needs with my own in the moment. Simply put, in order to grow happy children, I as a parent needed to monitor my own healthiness and continually grow and mature emotionally. Of course if you were raised in a healthy, wholesome home – this may not be a challenge for you like it had been for me and seems to be for many others. Some call it being an "adult-child", but whatever one calls it, it is realizing that we may have automatically grown older but we have not automatically "grown-up". I have found this to be at the root of many of the families I have counseled for problems in the parent-child relationship and thus suggest this as the place to start in developing parent leaders.

2. Steps to personal growth:

a.) Rebuilding self image

Sometimes we need to reflect on how we see ourselves and how that relates to being a parent. I encourage parents to examine their self image and if it is negative then the most important place to start changing our thinking is our thinking about ourselves and thereby creating a positive, healthy, whole self image. This can be challenging, to look within and do an autopsy of yourself to see what causes you to do and say things that we usually end up apologizing for (or at least should apologize for). However, this process is so important for parents in exercising the capacity to become self-aware by thinking about our thinking about ourselves. Oftentimes there are unresolved wounds, shame or guilt from our past that we discover have not been dealt with and are at the root of hindering healthy, happy relationships with our children.

"Hurting people, hurt people and are easily hurt by them"

– John Maxwell

The above statement is very simple, yet very telling as to what might cause us to hurt those closest to us and help bring the understanding of how we can hurt those we really love, like our children. Parents struggling with their children need to be encouraged to be intentional about this and not overlook or excuse their way out of the inner reflection that helps to produce emotional wholeness and maturity vital for good parenting.

"Sow a thought, reap an action. Sow an action,
reap a habit. Sow a habit, reap a character.
Sow a character, reap a destiny."
- Anonymous

The significance of this truth is powerful and can be a blessing or a curse depending on our understanding of it and making it work for us or against us. The Universe operates by the laws of nature and man can benefit from these laws, or be negatively impacted by these laws, whether or not he understands them. For example, the law of gravity is working right now, whether you understand it or not or are aware of it or not, it is holding you down. The same is true for the law of sowing and reaping. If I plant apple seeds, I will grow or reap apples. That is the law. If I plant lemon seeds, I will reap lemons. That is the law and so forth. Likewise, if I plant negative thoughts and actions, I will reap negative consequences in my life. However, if I plant good thoughts and actions, I will reap good things. That is the law and it never fails to work this way.

Go back to the quote above and think about it with this understanding. The point is we can control our destiny beginning with our thoughts, which lead to our actions, which turn into habits, which form our character, which leads us to our ultimate destiny and it all starts with taking control of my thought life mostly about myself.

As an exercise, take a few minutes to consider the following:

What kind of messages did you receive as a child from your parents (or other important adults in your childhood)? Consider both positive and negative messages. These messages were delivered by words or statements your parents said (and did not say) and things your parents did (and did not do).

Take a few minutes to write these down in your journal or personal diary. Begin to discipline your mind to catch and replace any negative thoughts about self with positive statements of self affirmation. For example, replace the thought; *"I'm just not cut out to be a good mother",* with; *"I am a good mother".* This will feel awkward at first, but with practice you will begin to feel more comfortable speaking these affirmations out loud to yourself. Initially you will feel as though you are lying to yourself, but you are not lying, but rather using the power of your words to replace negative thinking by "sowing" positive thoughts that will soon grow into actions, habits, character and destiny.

b.) The power of choice

> *"The last of human freedoms is the ability to choose*
> *one's attitude under any circumstances."*
> *–Victor Frankl, Man's Search for Meaning.*

Happy parents produce happy children. Sometimes the challenges of life can steal our joy, circumstances can overwhelm our emotions and unexpected adversity can completely disrupt everything. It is in those tough times that we often determine our quality of life because the choice really is ours to make. This idea is based on the philosophy that my state of mind or "being" is really not due to what happens to me, as much as what I decide to do about what happens to me. Or what I decide to do about how "I feel" about what happens to me, and how I decide to think about what happens to me. Victor Frankl wrote about his experience in the German concentration camps during the Holocaust, and he sought to understand why some were able to maintain hope and what impact that had. His conclusion in the quote above was about the power of choice.

As human beings, unlike animals, we can choose our thoughts and response to what happens to us, rather than being controlled by our feelings and acting instinctively like animals. This takes practice, but the fact is my feelings don't have to dictate my thoughts and reactions, I can choose to create my own reality. Thus, when it comes to raising my children and building my family life, I am not bound by my past hurts, but I can choose to overcome them and create a better life for my family.

c.) Forgiveness

"We must develop and maintain the capacity to forgive. He who is devoid of the power to forgive is devoid of the power to love. There is some good in the worst of us and some evil in the best of us. When we discover this, we are less prone to hate our enemies."

– Dr. Martin Luther King Jr.

A critical part of growing ourselves is identifying areas in our lives where forgiveness is needed. It is impossible to be a human being and not be hurt along the way. What we do with those hurts, however, is the key to whether the hurts make us a victim of them or a victor over them. The ability to forgive is a decision of our will. Some things are easier to forgive than others. Some people are easier to forgive than others. Just like any other skill or art, forgiveness must be learned, demonstrated, nurtured and continuously practiced. Have you ever noticed how much easier children will forgive? But as the years go by if forgiveness is not modeled and communicated by parents to their children when they do wrong, the heart begins to harden. Forgiveness becomes harder to practice and revenge, anger, guilt, and shame take root in their hearts. I can't tell you how many kids have sat in my office and cried as they told me that they thought their parents were still angry at them, months and years after the fact. They felt rejected, shameful, abandoned, and unforgiven. Love at home was based on performance instead of love that is unconditional. Others, who have attempted suicide, run away from home, joined gangs, tried sex, drugs, alcohol and dropping out of school expressed similar feelings, as did others who have confided in me the abuse they have endured in one form or another. What is the result of all this? A generation of violent hearts!

> *"I totally agree with your explanation and assessment as to why most young people join gangs. I have first hand experience of having joined a gang in my youth. I am now 65 years of age and have done time in three different prisons when young because of drinking early in life and being in gangs. I have stopped drinking and being in gangs since 1972 and forever! My father did not care about me and physically and emotionally abused me as a young boy. That made me an easy target for gang recruitment since I had no love at home I thought the gang would be my caring family. And since I was very angry at my father when the gang members asked me to join them I joined without hesitation."*
> *–Jose Cardona, author, "God's Awesome Redeeming Grace" (Outskirts press, 2007)*

There are no quick fixes, no easy solutions, and no magic formulas. There is however one thing I have seen that begins the process of a changed life and that is the personal experience of the love and forgiveness of God. I have dared to ask abused kids to forgive their parents, rape victims to forgive their perpetrators, and gang members to forgive their rivals. I wish I could say that my motive has been out of compassion for the perpetrator, but it is really more because of the freedom, the joy, and the peace I know forgiving brings to the victim. As I experienced the love and forgiveness of God it gave me the courage to forgive others. Years later after my father died, I remember I broke down crying and was able to forgive him for all the injustices and anger that was in my heart towards him for the things he'd done to my mother, my siblings and to me. I am no longer a victim tormented or controlled by my past. Forgiveness takes me from victim to victor! Although this is not an easy thing to do, the results of reconciliation are worth the struggle as we learn how to forgive even if the person is no longer in your life; it is still a very liberating life changing experience to forgive.

I realize acts of violence will continue and many young people will continue to be victims. What helps me from becoming overwhelmed or cynical is the saying by Henry David Thoreau, “For every thousand men hacking at the leaves of evil, there is one striking at the root.”. I believe teaching angry hearts to forgive strikes at the root of the evil of violence in our society. I am one turned heart who has helped turn others, who have helped turn others. Thus the one, over time, becomes the many on a mission to reach one more heart of violence and turn it into a heart of peace.

For more information on parent personal growth and leadership: www.RichardRRamos.com

CHAPTER 5

Twelve years to Gang Prevention

"My dad is the only parent I have and I don't know what I would do without him. He takes care of me and provides for me, he always has. I get to have a close relationship with him, and I know that he'll always be there to protect me...Father's are a vital part of life. I think they should be recognized more often"
-Gina Garrett, a teenage single Mom

Law enforcement and gang intervention practitioners know that studies on gangs and kids who join them tell us that most kids join gangs between the ages of 12-15. If that is the case, then the hopeful message for parents is that we have a twelve year window of opportunity to work in to produce happy, healthy children that will never have the desire to join a "second family" (gangs). When we break these twelve years down even further, we are really looking at three critical time frames for parents to work in the fertile ground of child development:

Infant – 2 years

Concentrate on your child's view of themselves:

Infants, toddlers and pre-school children in and of themselves have no concept of gangs, let alone the desire to join gangs. Thus, the parents are not competing with the lure of the "streets", media or peer pressure during these early formative years of a child's self-image. Parents have every advantage to "plant, cultivate and grow" in their children the character, self-esteem, sense of self-worth, confidence and all the other aspects of healthy human development with no outside competition.

2 years – 5 years

Concentrate on your child's view of respect for parental authority: These are critical years for balancing the healthy individual self-image with the proper discipline and respect for "others" that produces a healthy respect for parental authority, guidance, family loyalty and sense of community.

5 years – 12 years

Concentrate on your child's view of their role in the community: Heavy parental investment of time and money in helping children to discover their talents, develop their skills, and dream about their individual purpose, destiny and positive contribution to their family and community.

The importance of these time frames for child development cannot be overlooked or over emphasized in terms of preventing kids from joining gangs or any negative lifestyle. Studies on child development tell us that the first five years of a child's life are the most important as far as establishing the roots of character. Parents have such an advantage during these crucial years to lay a foundation from which a child will mature into a healthy, wholesome, happy individual equipped with the character to make the right choices and lead a positive life that avoids the paths to gangs and other negative lifestyles. In her book, *"How Children become Violent – Keeping your Kids out of Gangs, Terrorist Organizations, and Cults"*, author Katherine Seifert, Ph.D., says:

"Over the last three decades as a criminal justice and psychotherapist professional, I saw countless patients with either severe mental illnesses or histories of grotesquely violent behavior. As I asked them questions and delved into their pasts, it became clear that many, if not all, had experienced some level of childhood trauma in the form of neglectful, painful, or violent upbringings...could there be some link between childhood trauma and the inability to lead normal, productive lives, and have more empathy for others?...the majority of violent and sexual offenders...had histories of childhood abuse, neglect, traumatic loss of parents without sufficient substitute caregivers...I found that the reason my patients could not conform to the rules of society was because of unaddressed traumatic childhoods..."

The Parent as a Gardener

To help parents grasp the skills to produce healthy, happy children, I use the metaphor of a gardener. A gardener must not only be knowledgeable, but skillful in cultivating both the soil and seeds that produce the healthy life and growth of the plant. For our purposes here I will explain the basic tools and ingredients used by the gardener in growing his garden and relate these to the skills needed by parents in raising, or nurturing the growth of their children.

Hands – When dirt is soft and fertile, one only needs to use the hands to dig a hole to plant the seeds. I liken this to the fertile condition of the heart of an infant and the importance of touch, affection, kissing, hugging, and all the physical ways we handle an infant to give them a sense of security, care and the intuitive message of self-worth.

Seeds – The seeds are what contain the life, but in and of themselves cannot produce that life within without the mixture of the soil, water and sun. Likewise; the soil, water and sun cannot produce life without the seeds because none of them contain the life within. The life is in the seeds. I liken "seeds" to the words of parents. We must understand how very powerful our words are and the affect they have on a child's life positively or negatively. The scriptures say; "Death and life are in the power of the tongue" (Proverbs 18.21), and in many other places they teach the principle of the power of our words to affect change for the good or bad. Thus, we parents must learn to be very conscious of how we speak to our children, not only when they have done well, but more importantly during the times when they have done wrong. Here are some principles for parents to remember in speaking to their children in all circumstances:

- When children do the wrong thing, parents must do and say the right thing
- Pause and think before you speak words you will need to apologize for later
- Catch your kids doing good (not just the bad) and never assume you can complement their good behavior enough
- Daily words of encouragement are needed just as much as daily meals
- Always praise in public – especially around friends and relatives
- Always (or as much as possible) correct in private

- Express positive words of acceptance, rather than negative words like, “but it could have been better if…”, or, “next time you should”, etc.

Water – Anyone who has ever grown a plant knows that in order for a plant to grow and look healthy, the roots must be watered on a consistent basis. Dry, wilted and dying plants can always be revived with a healthy and consistent dose of watering the roots. I liken the roots of a plant to the soul of a child. The soul is the seat of our emotions, our thinking and our will, or ability to choose. The parent is the gardener of the soul of each of their children. We must take care to consistently “water the soul” so as not to allow it to dry, wilt and die. Some psychologists call this “soul sickness”. Others may refer to it as depression, withdrawal, shyness or shame. Whatever one calls it, it is unhealthy. There are many ways to water the soul, here are just a few:

- For the mind: read to and with the child, story telling, drawing, coloring, music, movies and other forms of using the imagination to stimulate the creative genius within each child. Watering the soul also includes building upon the ability to think, analyze, reason, use logic and all other aspects of building intellectual capacity.
- For the emotions: empathize, sympathize, cuddle, listen, and understanding. So many gang members I’ve spoken to expressed how sad they were that they were unable to talk to their parents, their parents did not “get it” (understand them) and never apologized when they were wrong, etc. Oftentimes all our children need is a listening ear and a hug, rather than a talking head and physical distance
- For the will: fair but firm discipline. Role models of trust, loyalty, self sacrifice, and compassion for others. Forgiveness, empathy, wisdom, knowledge, and all other attributes that help a child learn to make “right” choices.

Shovel – the shovel is a tool used to break up or till the soil in preparation to receive the planted seeds. I liken this to the parent being skillful in the use of discipline. Discipline is dealing with the heart of a child to prepare them to receive instruction, wisdom and understanding of a needed life lesson that will benefit them later in life. The renowned child psychologist, Dr. James Dobson, speaks about the "strong-willed child" and the need for parents to learn how to "bend the child's will without breaking their spirit". Another way of understanding this skill is to think of a musician who must always be fine tuning their instrument each time they play it. With a guitar, if the musician pulls the string too hard it will break, if he does not pull it tight enough it will be out of tune. And no matter how many times an instrument is tuned up, it always needs to be tuned up before it can play at peak potential. This skill of "just enough" is what we as parents must learn in the use of discipline.

The term "discipline" comes from the Latin word "disciplinare," which means "to teach." Many people, however, associate the word with only the idea of punishment, which falls short of the full meaning of the word. Discipline, properly practiced, uses a multifaceted approach, including models, rewards, and punishments that teach and reinforce desired behavior. Through discipline, children are able to learn self-control, self-direction, competence, and a sense of caring.

Principles for exercising discipline include:

- Removing privileges that a child enjoys
- Isolation through timeouts
- Verbal reprimand

What about "spanking"? – Some will, some won't – but for those who will, it must be properly done. How? – Here are a few guidelines:

- Parents should explain for which behavior the child is being spanked
- With small children using the hand for one or two swats on the bottom is sufficient.
- For older children (5-10) a designated paddle can be used for a swat on the bottom.
- Parents should talk about the behavior some time later to bring understanding, reconciliation and closure.
- Slapping, punching, kicking, beating and any other form of physical force that is physically harmful to the child is abuse and never acceptable. What is proper spanking? Spanking on the bottom - nothing more, nothing less.

When should the use of spanking end? – In general, once a child reaches the age of 12, or, "age of accountability", other forms of discipline are better suited that recognize the growth and maturity of the child who is beyond the spanking stage.

I realize how controversial this issue is and many of you reading this will disagree with spanking children for any reason. Yet, we must respect the fact that many parents do in fact use this as a form of discipline for their children. Furthermore, many parents are under the false assumption that it is illegal to spank children. Spanking is not illegal (though some states are making an effort to outlaw it) and this fact needs to be clarified. What's illegal is physically abusing children. Spanking, in and of itself, should not be confused with physical abuse. Nevertheless, guidance is required for parents who do spank their children to ensure they understand the difference and practice this form of discipline properly. To be clear, I am not making an argument for right or wrong on the issue, but rather making the case, for parents who choose to spank, it should be done properly and we should not assume all parents are doing it properly, nor expect them to stop just because others are against it.

Shears – pruning shears is a tool a gardener uses to train a plant, shape a plant and cause the plant to grow back bigger and stronger seasonally. Again, this takes knowledge of the needs and peculiar growth patterns of each individual type of plant. Some plants need pruning during the winter, others need trimming all year long and so forth. Children are much the same way. No two are alike and a parent must tend to the particular needs and temperament of each child, thus sending a strong message of value for their individuality. This also speaks to the parent being aware of the different phase they are now in as a "coach" of their child watching from the sidelines of life and providing guidance from a distance, but always close enough to give counsel as needed.

Based on this understanding, below are six principles I teach young people and encourage all parents to use as guidelines for similar instruction with their children:

- Teach children their life is not an accident

- Teach children they have a significant role to play in society
- Teach children their life is a reward to parents, not a burden
- Help children discover the gifts and talents "hidden" in them – They don't have to invent their life as much as discover it
- Help your child develop their natural talents
- Teach and prepare your child for their destiny in society

For more information on how to use these parenting skills visit: www.RichardRRamos.com

CHAPTER 6

Parental Authority

"Authority without wisdom is like a heavy ax without an edge: fitter to bruise than to polish"

- Anne Bradstreet

When parents ask me what the best way is to prevent their small children from joining gangs, I reply by telling them to focus on the following three things:

1. Teach your children to respect your authority
2. Begin with teaching them to accept "No" for an answer
3. Teach them to accept the "No" answer without an attitude

There are long term benefits from raising our children to be obedient. It seems that some of these terms like; authority, control, obedience and submission of children to parents have become politically incorrect amongst many, but, in general, the "fruit" speaks for itself when objectively measuring the results and productivity of those kids raised under their parents loving, guiding authority vs. those left to themselves and their own autonomy.

In this life, anything can happen to anybody at anytime as seems to be the case all too often as senseless accidents and unusual events that end up taking lives, or damaging future potential, have touched us all in one way or another. Having said that, it seems there are greater consequences for children who never seem to learn to accept that little word, "no" from their parents. After all, what really is the difference between a youth out late beyond their curfew, and at greater risk for danger, and those who have come home on time, or decide not to go out at all? Often the only difference was obedience to the word of parental authority that said, "No, you can't stay out longer", or "No, you can't go out". Parents must understand the power of this little word and the ramifications of not teaching their children to respect it, accept it and obey it. How many teens have suffered consequences they now regret simply because they refused to accept the authority of a parent who said "no"? Even more tragically, how many families are agonizing today over a life changing tragedy that might have been avoided if their child had just accepted their answer of "no"?

Why is it that kids will not accept "no" from their parents? Some of it is a normal part of growing up. Another part is a result of something that was not learned as a child and is now manifesting as a loss of respect for their parents' authority. It's not a lack of love for their parents, or that their parents are always wrong, but it is a normal part of them that wants to rebel against a higher authority that is not allowing them to have what they want, when they want it, a symptom of a battle that was lost years ago by many parents. This disobedience is rooted in contempt for the authority of parents and must not be ignored. The consequences are too great, the heartaches too painful, the arguments too draining and the emotional exhaustion too unhealthy. Thus, as a measure of prevention, parents must teach small children to accept "no" for an answer to inappropriate behavior, wants and desires. This is a battle that must be won! It is a battle that must be handled correctly, consistently, fairly and firmly. In addition, the second aspect to this important principle of accepting "no" for an answer is teaching children to accept it without an attitude. Many parents tend to make the mistake of allowing their children to outwardly obey their "no", but neglect to deal with the inner attitude of their reluctant obedience. This reminds me of the story of the father who got into a confrontation with his child during a church service as the child refused sit down. After arguing back and forth, the little boy finally obeyed after his father, who threatened to spank him if he did not sit down, to which the boy replied, "I might be sitting down on the outside, but on the inside I am still standing up!".

This describes many situations in our home today. We may get our kids to outwardly conform, but we overlook that inwardly (where true respect and obedience lie) they are not transformed. Thus, when they get old enough and big enough our threats are no longer a threat to them and they disrespect, defy and disobey our parental authority. When parents are unaware of this inner defiance they often mistakenly reward it and reinforce this behavior. For example, a parent says "no" to their child for some reason and the child reluctantly obeys, but cops an attitude along with it. This is usually manifested by them making life miserable for everyone else in the house, especially younger siblings, by angrily slamming doors or doing chores given for punishment by throwing things and giving half an effort, having a long face and short, angry answers for others in the house, etc. Nonetheless, the parent got the outward obedience and decides to leave the attitude alone. The next day, Tia (Spanish for aunt) so and so calls and offers to take the kids for an outing. Now the child is begging to go and reminding the reluctant parent that they "obeyed" – "I did what you told me to do yesterday" and the parent, wanting to be on good terms again, reasons in their mind, "well, she did do what I asked", and gives permission to go.

This is a common occurrence as most parents know. We have all given in to the pressure of family dropping by at the wrong time with an invitation to do something fun, etc. But, what we have really done by giving in is reward this inner, defiant attitude and missed the opportunity to properly enforce consequences for coping the attitude so that the child can learn that accepting "no" with an attitude is not acceptable. We have also demonstrated to younger siblings that they too don't have to take us serious either, as long as they outwardly obey they will still get to do the fun things.

This short example may seem like a stretch to some, but the bottom line is that this happens much too often and the kids don't learn the lesson and parents will not gain the respect and inward obedience they seek unless they are consistent in bringing consequences both for wrong behavior and a wrong attitude for the consequences for the wrong behavior. Children must be brought into a healthy understanding that outward conformity with an inner attitude of defiance is unacceptable and that consequences are still in force until the inner attitude is transformed into a sincere apology and a rightful respect for authority. *I cannot over emphasize just how important this point is as a key to gang prevention that is so often overlooked, not understood or insisted upon as a vital parent leadership principle in raising happy, healthy children!*

As stated earlier, how to go about disciplining children to teach them respect for parental authority is controversial business these days. But it must be done and each family will have to determine what form of discipline works best for them. Many parents struggle between being too permissive and being too strict, whether to spank or not, but the point is that it is through consistent, firm and fair discipline that parents can build the character in their children. This gives them the inner strength and conviction of right from wrong and how to give “no” as an answer to their friends under pressure and in the tough environment that kids find themselves in today. This does not mean that children will always do what is right or make the right decision and never give into peer pressure. It does mean that you at least have helped prepare them and given them the tools to make good choices most of the time over a lifetime.

For more information on parental training in this area please visit: www.RichardRRamos.com

CHAPTER 7

Mentors for Parents

Youth are not our future, healthier Parents are!

It is often said that our youth are the future and we are encouraged along with schools, government, social programs and businesses to "invest" in our youth. While I do believe there is some truth to this thinking, I have to disagree with the notion that only "youth" are our future and suggest that it is really us "parents" who are in the best position to affect "our future". Yet, today's parents struggle as much or more in raising children as they did in the past and thus the need for parent mentors as well as youth mentors. In 1987 Dr. James Dobson, a child psychologist, took a poll of 35,000 parents that showed *the number one feeling among parents was "guilt and failure".* More recently, as I have spoken with and counseled hundreds of parents myself, I still found similar feelings of confusion, anger, frustration, emotional exhaustion, depression, hopelessness, shame, and a loss of confidence. One result of this is that more and more children are being left to themselves, as discouraged parents give up their struggle for authority in their children's life and we are all paying a heavy price for it. In so many of the homes I have visited the parents are there physically, but there is no respect for their authority. When parents lose their position of authority in the home it only adds to other adult pressures that we face emotionally, financially and socially. Without proper order, understood roles, and lack of cooperation, our homes become another battleground to fight on instead of being a refuge to flee to after a long day of work.

One of the battlegrounds a growing number of parents, especially immigrant parents, are losing their children to is the culture in our schools and neighborhoods. Having worked on school campuses, I can say that some school campus cultures can in many ways cultivate rebellion, defiance of authority, violence, sexual promiscuity, drug and alcohol use and a lack of motivation to name a few. This culture, that parents are demanded by law to send their kids to each morning, is often times working against them in more ways than they realize and they come home to this "culture war" daily. Most parents don't want to give up the battle, but neither do they know what to do, how to do it, where else to turn, or what else to try. There is also a growing number of single parents, teen parents, and what I call "GXG's, which stands for "generation X grandparents" who are parents in their 30's and 40's, that have become grandparents and are raising their kids and their kids, kids! Again, I understand what most people mean when they say that we must invest in our youth because they are our future, but the real need for investment is in mentors for today's parents and grandparents. They need intervention, and more mentoring in parental leadership, and they need it now or more of our youth will be lost to our increasing number of jails, prisons and grave yards!

I believe, rather, I know, that every kid desires to love, respect, and obey his or her parents. Many gang members have shared this with me themselves, during those moments when I have been able to have that "heart to heart" conversation with them. They are oftentimes only acting in a way that allows survival and/or are choosing behavior based on their interpretation of some of the confrontations they have had with their parents, but have never talked about. Some actually think that their parents are still mad at them, dislike them, or love their younger or "good" siblings more. The message they get is that they are no longer wanted at home or valued as an important member of the family because of some of the mistakes and bad choices they have made. The fact is parents are often times guilty of making mistakes or bad choices in how we have handled the bad choices of our children. I suggest this is at the root of most broken child-parent relationships, and the area where parents need training in how to do the necessary work to win the respect of their children and gain the proper authority in their child's life. Let's not put the responsibility of our future in the hands of our children, but rather let's work together to train more parent mentors who produce more parents on a mission dedicated to becoming healthier parents!

Below are three principles I suggest:

1. Decide that a good relationship is more important than just being "right".

As parents we must set the example of humility to our kids. We must be willing to re-think what we have done. The words we used, the way we reacted to a difficult situation. Even after we re- think it all, we may still conclude that we were "right". But this is not enough, or the important point, because our child has not accepted our position and is obviously upset about something. At this point many parents take the attitude of "too bad, they will just have to get over it". But oftentimes they don't. Instead they harbor resentment and begin to disrespect us as "adults". Not because they think they are always right, but because we do. Usually, kids know when they are in the wrong, so what they are reacting to is our disrespect for their views and a valuing of their development process as teenagers. After all, didn't most of us make the same mistakes? Does that have something to do with our negative, intolerant reaction? Are we more concerned with our image as parents with others, than we are with the natural growth process of our children? Isn't the more important issue the fact that our child is not happy with how we have handled their mistakes? What are we going to do with that? At this juncture, I suggest that we need to think beyond who is right or wrong, and consider if there was not a better way to handle the situation allowing our kids to maintain their sense of self- respect, without side stepping the issue of wrong behavior.

Perhaps we need to go back and listen a little more to their side of things and make them feel understood, even if we don't agree. All of this is done because we want to have a good relationship and maintain our role as the prime authority figures in their lives. Experience tells me that most kids will respond to this type of exercising our authority and that they will respect us for our humility, fairness and willingness to hear them out. The bottom line is the clear message we are sending them that we value them as individuals and want a healthy and meaningful relationship with them that goes beyond just always having to be right.

2. Admit when you are wrong and apologize

Once I practiced the "art of listening", both with my own kids and those I have worked with over the years, I discovered that I was often wrong in my thoughts, words and deeds, plain and simple, no excuses or explanations. It was usually a result of jumping to conclusions and/or reacting out of anger. I discovered I was wrong in two ways. First, my conscience was bothering me in the way in which I had handled the situation. Second, I went back with more control of my anger and listened. As my kids tearfully would explain how they felt and explained their reasoning and views, only my pride would keep me from admitting to myself, and to them, that I was in the wrong. Usually my error was in the way I handled the situation, and sometimes in my judgment of the situation, yet both called for the humility to say that I was wrong, apologize and ask for forgiveness.

After my three oldest children (five in all) had become teenagers I felt the need to apologize for some of the mistakes I had made with them as I was in a time of personal growth and could see that they were beginning to resent the way their younger siblings were benefiting from my growth. I was more patient, understanding, lenient and flexible. We had a short meeting and I began to share my heart and apologize for what they had to experience with a younger and less experienced father. I was not abusive, but overly strict and intolerant in ways that I knew had probably bruised their hearts in some ways. As I turned to my oldest son (who is my step-son, but whom I have raised since he was two years old) and apologized for disciplining him too harshly at times, he began to break down and cry. Not until that moment did I realize how much I had bruised his heart and that he obviously had been carrying this in his heart. I could feel and see that a healing was taking place in his heart towards me and all I could do was hug him, cry and apologize. We always had a good relationship, but after this I know it was deepened and better than ever before and remains so today.

I cannot remember a time that this sincere humility demonstrated to either gang members I was working with or with my own children, was rejected and did not elicit the same admission from them of their wrong and the offering of an apology. When children witness authority figures admit to their mistakes and apologize for them, it goes along way in establishing a respect for you and ultimately your authority.

3. Be Flexible, Fair and Firm

The ability of parents to be flexible in exercising their authority gives them a great deal of credibility and favor with their growing children. It symbolizes that you recognize they are growing up, are willing to bend the rules as a form of allowing them to earn trust and demonstrates that you understand that the "spirit" of the law is more important than the "letter" of the law. What has helped me with this aspect is to know the difference between mistakes or accidents and defiance or willful disobedience. As parents we can sometimes be guilty of "choking on the ant, but swallowing the camel". In other words, we make the little things big things and the big things little. And for some reason, kids are very tuned in to this kind of unfairness or injustice and have a keen sense of what is a mountain and what is a mole hill. This is why it is a good practice to include your kids (10 years and older) in deciding what the consequences are for both good and bad behavior. Many times I was pleasantly surprised at the punishment they deemed for themselves as I was not going to be as strict as they were on themselves. But, we agreed to their terms and they were respectful of "our" decision. I think the key here is that kids know that you have the final word, yet you are allowing them to judge themselves and this is where you can gain respect, earn loyalty and create emotional bonds that pay big dividends later on down the road when it counts. There are times when one must be firm, and there are times when mercy and grace are called for and the wise parent will learn when to exercise them in a timely manner. This takes perception, insight, knowledge, and experience but it also requires the ability to listen to your kids to learn how to discern different situations. Through being flexible, fair and firm we open up the opportunities to develop character, increase the level of the relationship and cease moments for a lesson in leadership and the proper use of authority.

CHAPTER 8

Tapping into gang Loyalty

I came from a very close knit family. I am an only child, so it was always just me, my mom and my dad. My father was an alcoholic or another term, a functioning drunk. I grew up in a neighborhood that was low class and was known as gang territory. My grandparents were Pachuco's, so I grew up knowing about the life.

I started "just hanging" around gang members when I was 8 years old. I quickly started feeling like a little family, which I was not feeling at home, so that felt real good. By the age of 10 I went to my first party with gang members. I liked how much fun I was having hanging out with my new "family" and in the mean while telling my parents I was with friends from school.

At the age of 11 I got jumped into the gang. I was jumped for 2 minutes by four 16 year old guys from my gang. At the age of 11, I took one hell of a beating...So now I was "in the gang." What does that really mean? I thought that night. Feeling accepted and wanted all the time? People not hurting me anymore because I now have new respect?

Boy was I WRONG! At the age of 12 I did my first drive by. Here I am as scared as can be in a car full of gang members (like me) going to do a drive by. That same year I had 5 homeboys die. That's when my grades in school started going down. My mom would ask what was going on with me. I kept explaining nothing. I was an undercover gang member to my parents. I blinded them with this good girlie act. My mom would say that I was dressing and looking like a "chola." I kept reassuring her that I was just dressing like one, because I like the style. My parents didn't want to admit that there little girl could be in a gang.

When I was 14 years old I was stabbed in the leg by a rival gang. So I thought that's all right because I "took one" for my neighborhood... (Yeah right!). All my friends were getting pregnant and having kids at 11, 12, 13 etc...By the time I was 18 years old I had 7 miscarriages. I cannot tell you how many times I heard the words "Oh baby I love you, its me and you forever." I learned real quick guys will tell you ANYTHING to get what they want. I had my closest home girls sleep with my man behind my back. (Good friends huh?)

By the time I was 18 I had lost 46 friends to gang violence. That's one hell of a lot of funerals to go to and a lot of innocent families to look into thier eyes and say sorry, when down deep inside they are cussing you out because they feel that you are just some gang member that helped him get in that casket. When I was 19 I was cruising with my homies... We were at a stop light. A rival gang drove up on us and shot at us. The guy that was driving was hit in the head and the bullet came out the other side of his head and ricocheted off my head. His brains were splattered all over me...After that I was shot at about a dozen times more. Then when I was 20 I was arrested for homicide... By the Grace of God, they found out that they had the wrong person. I was never so scared in my life...going to jail for something I didn't do for the rest of my life. So I prayed and prayed. The Lord heard my prayers. After that I thought I owe this to God that I am alive. I owe it to myself and my loved ones to stay alive.

At 21 I decided that I had enough. So one night I was kicking back in my neighborhood. There were about 50 of us that night. I told them I wanted out. I said if you want to jump me out then that is fine, but I want out. I went and talk to one of the Veteranos (older homeboys).They said "You did yours for the neighborhood and you can just walk out with respect because we have respect for you." As I was getting ready to leave and saying bye to everyone... The police rolled up and I thought "I guess one last time." So there I was on the floor, on my knees, hands behind my head and an officer behind me with a 12 gauge shot gun to the back of my head...These cops who ran the gang unit knew me by name. That night I told them that I was out of the scene. They congratulated and even gave me hugs. Then asked if I needed a ride home. That was the first time I was in a police car without hand cuffs on.

I saw a lot of friends die for my neighborhood, but what does a neighborhood do for you?

You claim a street or hood that you will NEVER own. You pay rent for a neighborhood that will NEVER be yours. I think now about all the funerals where everyone said they would die for there homie, but you know I never seen anyone jump on the casket and go in the ditch with them. When you take a life or have one taken from you, it affects more then just you.

If you are a gang member PLEASE take it from me there is a REAL life out there. You just have to be strong enough to take a chance and walk away before it is too late. Life is too short anyways...then to let it be even more shortened by doing time in prison or being dead. If you live a real Gangsters life that is the only two ways out, prison or death. There are so many other things out there in life for you.

If you don't care enough about yourselves to get out STOP being SELFISH and think about all the loved ones you will leave behind. How will they handle life without a husband, wife, brother, sister, daughter, son, mother, and father. Pictures, memories and a cemetery is all they will have left. PLEASE think about it!!!

One of the lessons we learn from this former gang member (and most overlooked qualities of gang members) is the sense of loyalty and deep commitment to their "homies" (Latino slang for best friends). This loyalty is misdirected, we would all agree, but that is not the point. The point is that it is present and it would do us well to focus our attention to that innate quality in all of our children, the desire and capacity to belong and to be loyal to what you belong to.

I grew up in North East Los Angeles, the territory of many Latino gangs from Highland Park, El Sereno, Boyle Heights, Cypress Park, Lincoln Heights, Eagle Rock, and the like. What I learned early in life was that belonging to a gang was normal, exciting, fun, and cool, but most importantly, it was about commitment, heart, loyalty to the hood and the homeboys. All for one and one for all, you had their back and they had yours anywhere, anybody, anytime. If there is one thing people know about gang members, it is their willingness to go to jail, prison, and even die for their hood and homies. We can criticize this and talk all we want, but the fact remains that there is something inside each of these young men and women that should be admired and that is their heart-felt loyalty to something bigger than they are. Growing up in this culture you learn that it's not about "I" and "mine", but ""we" and "ours". That's what the graffiti was all about, the tattoos, the dress, the cars, the slang, the drugs, the booze, the cruising, the ditching school and the fights. It was about "being down", being loyal to the hood and homies. It was all we knew and who we were and we were proud of our identity.

This loyalty is found in every gang and gang member and is something we can work with in our efforts to prevent young men and women giving their loyalty to someone else and something else. The question is, why? Why do they want to give their loyalty to a gang? The answer to that question is hard to swallow for many parents, but it is one we should explore if we hope to restore that loyalty to its proper place and win back our youth from the dangers of the gang banging lifestyle. What we as parents can learn and come to understand is that every child desires, and has an ability to give this loyalty to them if they are willing to pay the price to earn it. This then gives our children the strength to say "no" to the gang because the gang is asking for a loyalty that they have already given away to their "first" family.

As the above story taught us, misplaced loyalty is a rude awakening. Many gang members are eventually disappointed and realize that they gave themselves to a false sense of love, security, and loyalty. Many who have gone on to juvenile hall, jail or prison discover that their "homies" are not as faithful as they thought they were. They find their girlfriends now going out with their friends and receive few if any letters, phone calls or visits. I have received many letters from young guys I know who ended up in prison and asked if I would write them because they were lonely and not hearing much from their friends and family on the outside. I also noticed this lack of loyalty when I was a correctional officer in two prisons and discussed the disappointment and betrayal these former street gang members felt from their "homies". This is often discouraging enough to cause a gang member to "wake up" and begin to consider leaving the gang behind.

Here is an example in a letter I received from a young man I have known since he was a child of twelve. As he grew older he became a gang member, made some wrong choices and found himself serving a sentence of sixteen years to life. He wrote this letter from prison, asking me to share with the youth I was working with at the time:

> *"I thought gang banging was the answer to the loneliness I felt inside. I thought drugs could take me out of the reality of life…let me tell you something you should know if you don't know already, the so called friends you have aren't your friends. I know from a firsthand basis. They're only there to use you for what you have because I was the same way in one way or another. It took me to lose my mom and my so called life I was living and to lose my loved ones. Don't let this happen to you and don't say it can't happen to you because you would be lying to yourself…"*
> *- Mark*

The message for us parents is that if a loyal, hard core gang member is turned off by mistrust to the point of leaving the gang, how much more would they want to "come home" to parents who have continued to reach out with unconditional love? However, the larger question is one of prevention and how to win our children's loyalty in the first place to prevent them from ever giving their loyalty to another "family"? One way I suggest is for parents to strive to become "Heroes".

CHAPTER 9

Parents as Heroes

". . . We cannot live fully without heroes, for they are the stars to guide us upward. They are the peaks on our human mountains. Not only do they personify what we can be, but they also urge us to be. Heroes are who we can become, if we diligently pursue our ideas ...Heroes are those who have changed history for the better...Their deeds are not done for the honor, but for the duty..."

–Frank Smith

Perhaps nothing has given me more joy as a father than to hear from each one of my children, at one time or another, that I am their hero. This is not because I have been perfect, or because I have always been the understanding, patient, morally good person behind closed doors. I believe it is because I have been honest, humble, admitted when I was wrong and asked for forgiveness. Of course it also has something to do with being good, moral, understanding when they failed, and supportive in the good and bad times, etc. Parents should understand that being the hero of our children is a noble and worthy goal to strive for and one we can attain without having to do everything right all the time.

Honesty with kids is a powerful tool of winning their hearts and loyalty.

And as we combine it with the other tools of moral character; understanding, forgiveness and trustworthiness, we can expect big dividends. Moreover, it will bring many happy moments in our relationships with our kids and earn their love and respect in ways that will help prevent them from joining gangs. I did not say it would prevent them from ever making bad decisions, choices or acting in ways that are negative. None of us could hold to that standard. However, I do believe that this notion of striving to be the hero of our children will prevent them from joining a gang or indulging in the negative "lifestyle" all parents want their children to avoid. I believe, overtime, parental moral character (which is the secret to moral authority) will win over the temptation of kids to give their loyalty elsewhere almost every time. When faced with peer pressure and hard decisions of social acceptance, most kids whose parents have been loyal to them emotionally and spiritually, will make the right moral choices because of their loyalty to the guidance and security of their parents, which have become their heroes; mom and dad, or whomever is in the role of parent, whether it be a single mom and/or a grandparent. This does not mean we'll avoid all problems or that some of our kids may not go astray for a season or two. But, over time, we will reap the harvest of the positive, loving seeds we planted in their fertile hearts as children!

I believe in heroes and the need for heroes in all of our lives as a source of inspiration and modeling of life that we can follow and draw strength from in our time of need. I define a "Hero" as someone bigger than life, someone to look up to, someone who is what I want to be, someone who does great things to help others, someone who I can trust and depend upon to always be there when I need them and someone who is loved by all. Now, I know I have just described "Superman/woman", but that is what a hero is in a sense. An almost mythical, mystery kind of a person, beyond the ordinary, unlike the rest of us, or so we think anyway and somehow it almost doesn't matter whether it is true or not or whether they really exist or not because we can still draw inspiration from this figure we have in our heart and mind as a personal source of inspiration.

It seems like today the heroes of our children are the rock star, movie star and athletic star. Yet, there was a time when the heroes of children in this country were NOT the movie star, rock star and sports star. This is not to say that all of the above people are not good role models, but then again, many parents do not want their kids to follow the "off screen" or "off the field" lifestyle of many of today's celebrity "heroes". As a professional in their field, there are many great actors, musicians, vocalist and athletes whose public performance can be awesome. However, what I am talking about is character, which can be defined as; what a person is in the dark when no one is looking. Personality and public performance have their place, especially when it comes to the entertainment field, but I am talking about the kind of hero who has character and moral authority all the time, or at least most all of the time, and not just as an actor on television.

I remember when the famous National Basketball Association (NBA) star, Charles Barkley, was in his heyday and he made the public comment to youth that he was not their role model. Barkley took a lot of flak for that statement and was chided by many as being irresponsible because the public expects star athletes to be and act as role models, which is a kind of hero, on and off the field. "Of course you are a role model Charles, you are my kids hero", they were essentially saying. But I think Mr. Barkley was misunderstood in the message he was trying to convey to both kids and parents especially. What I made of Barkley's' point, was that he was not the person kids should be looking up to just because he was a good basketball player that they did not know personally. While he admitted that he did not want that type of responsibility for his public and private life, his main point was that it is the parents' kids should look up to, who may not be able to dunk a basketball, hit a homerun, throw a football seventy yards or set an Olympic record of some kind. But rather, they work day in and day out and sacrifice to be involved in their children's lives. They are the true role models and heroes kids should be honoring. I couldn't agree more. The National Cable Sports Station, ESPN, has run commercials that depict pro athletes honoring and mobbing the normal parent or worker as a celebrity, and thus sending a message to the fans about who is really important in society, which are parents and the "ordinary guy" just doing his regular job. These are who should really receive the public attention and not be overlooked as a heroic symbol of character, work ethic, commitment and morality.

I imagine that many of you reading this today would agree that when you think back to who it was you looked up to and wanted to be like, it was your own mom and dad. Thus, I strongly urge today's parents to think deeply and seriously consider this notion of themselves as heroes to their children. Emerson said, *"A hero is no braver than an ordinary man, but he is braver five minutes longer".*

As parents we learn our duty to our children. And as we stumble here and there at times and perhaps think little of the little things we do for our kids, those are the very things that often cause us to be heroes in their eyes. You might be saying, "That's a big ball to carry", yes it is, but it is one we must pick up since it has been dropped by so many parents. There are many aspects about being a hero, but for now I want to share just three basic principles in the making of a hero that I believe are foundational for every parent, step-parent, and future parent in becoming the hero of their children:

- First, is the power of choice. The choice of investing their time in their children as first, important, and top priority.
- Second is the character of personal leadership. We don't have to be perfect, just honest to win the love and respect of our children, and humble enough to apologize when we make mistakes.
- Third is the hour of "their" crisis. It may not seem important to us, or like a crisis to us, but if it is important to them, or a crisis in their eyes, in those hard times we just show up. We may not have all the answers or know the right words to speak, but we can show up in the crisis of life and often times that is all that is needed.

Every era has those extraordinary men and woman who have risen to the challenges of their time. It is my contention that the extraordinary men and woman of our time who must rise up to take on the complex challenge of "gang prevention" at this time, more than any other single entity, institution or community program, are parents. That's why I call them; "Parents on a Mission!" I believe that gang prevention/intervention funds must be rewarded to help reproduce more parents who silently, consistently, and relentlessly provide that stable, secure and loving home in the midst of all the distractions that are pulling our children out of the home and on to the streets.

Gang prevention is not a matter of keeping our children from ever being touched by any negative experience available in today's gang culture. No, our challenge is not one of isolation but one of infiltration. Infiltrating the hearts and homes of the hopeless with parent heroes! As one minister put it, *"What counts in life is not being a hero to a guy two thousand miles away, but being a hero to a kid who is nine years old two bedrooms away."*

PART II

GANG INTERVENTION

CHAPTER 10

INTERVENTION THROUGH RECONCILIATION

"Never walk away from failure. On the contrary, study it carefully and imaginatively for its hidden assets"
- Michael Korda

In my view, the most effective way to intervene and give immediate help to those parents who are losing, or have lost their kids to street gangs or other negative lifestyles, is by coaching them in how to reconcile broken relationships and re-establish important practices of parenting they have lost in one way or another. The breakdown in relationship is due to several factors. In most cases, it has to do with some part of the following four general areas:

1. **A loss of Respect–Due to a lack of exercising proper discipline**
   What I found in the majority of cases, were good parents who did not know how to discipline their children to respect their authority. Or, in some cases, had abused their authority, which resulted in a loss of respect and they did not know how to gain it back.

2. **A loss of Influence–Due to a lack of understanding**
   As our children grow, we must also grow with them. Too many parents want to use the kind of control with their teenagers that they

used on them when they were little children. This attitude causes the old "generation gap", which is a result of refusing to see our world of yesterday through the lenses of our children's view of today and tomorrow. Thus, our children become influenced more by those they feel understand them and value their views, which are usually their school and neighborhood friends, which are not always the kind of influence parents want for their children. While it is challenging for parents to hold the dual position of authority and also be one who "understands", it is possible if we are willing to work at it.

3. **A loss of Relationship–Due to a lack of communication**

   I found this to be more prevalent among fathers, than with the mothers. The ability to look our children in the eyes and affirm them, share our hearts as men, and to verbally admit when we are wrong, say we are sorry, and ask to be forgiven. This was another common theme I heard among the kids, the fact that their parents "never" admitted when they were wrong. Sometimes as parents we can be so concerned with being right that we win the argument but don't realize that we have lost the relationship! To build healthy relationships with our children sometimes hangs on the ability to say the following words: I was wrong, I am sorry, please forgive me and I love you.

4. **A loss of Trust–Due to immorality**

   We parents must understand the affect our immorality has upon our children. Immorality, by those in authority, is usually interpreted as abuse of authority. This has caused a lot of mistrust and negativity towards the concept of authority as a whole. However, we should remember that having authority does not place us above mistakes and failure and we should readily admit our failures and own up to the consequences. When used properly, authority serves as a great source of providing children security, value, safe boundaries, and liberation. But when immorality as a lifestyle is prevalent in the home, kids tend to lose their feeling of security, as well as, their trust in the parent or parents engaged in such behaviors.

Parents often do not recognize their loss of the above. For example, parents expect to have positional authority or appointed authority that is automatically respected by their children. However, as parents we cannot suddenly demand respect for our authority from our teenagers, if we did not earn it from them when they were children. This is a common mistake many parents make, especially when they begin to realize that they are losing control of their kids. Often times the reason for this is that we did not understand our need to "earn" respect and obedience, since we could physically and psychologically control our little children. We knew that we could "scare" them or "bribe" them into obedience. But as kids grow physically and mentally, we find that these methods of fear, intimidation and bribery are no longer effective.

The path to restoring these things is not an easy one, nor is it a short process. It will take time, patience, diligence, and discipline. For this reason, many are not willing to pay the price of gaining back what they have lost in their children. "It's too hard", or, "It's too late", some say and they become discouraged. However, the loss of relationship and living through the gang membership of your children will be harder.

At this point, I want to share a word of encouragement to those parents whose kids are already in a gang and it's breaking your heart:

Take a moment to think, reflect, meditate or pray and be encouraged to allow for the desire and love you have for your children to provide you with the motivation you need to work through this process until you achieve the desired result. If you have lost your child for the reasons I've described thus far, take heart. It is possible for you to restore your relationship and see your child "come home" physically, emotionally and spiritually. I have seen it happen many times and the patience and work involved is well worth the effort. You will need help, especially if you are a single parent. This is precisely what this book and my POM curriculum is all about.

CHAPTER 11

TURNING THE HEARTS

"Too often we underestimate the power of
a touch, a smile, a kind word, a listening ear,
an honest compliment, or the smallest act of caring,
all of which have the potential to turn a life around"
- Leo Buscaglia

Effective intervention involves the work of helping violent youth resolve the issues that are deeply embedded in their angry hearts, and thus the term; "Turning the hearts". I suggest that violent acts are the result of an angry heart. Think about it. If you have ever acted violently or witnessed violent acts, what was the emotional state you were in? Isn't it true that someone acting violently is not calm inside? I know that whenever I acted violently it was easy because of all the pent up anger I was carrying around inside. But what causes an angry heart? Again, I suggest an angry heart is the result of unresolved injustices. I am sure all of us have felt the indignation or anger that rises up within us as we read about, hear about, or witness injustice. Anger is a God-given endowment that is to be used for the right purposes of self defense or defending the helpless in adverse circumstances. The metaphor of mama bear coming to the rescue of baby bear in an angry violent confrontation to save her cubs life shows the proper use of anger. But what happens in the human heart when injustice goes unresolved? The result is a heart full of hurt, resentment, bitterness and anger. In working with and counseling hundreds of youth and families I heard the many sad stories explain how these injustices are suffered in the home. When we understand what causes an angry heart, we can work to heal those hearts and bring hope to many parents whose kids are committing acts of violence.

In the book, "Kids Who Kill" (Ewing, Avon Bocks, New York, 1996) they found that the number one factor among teenagers that have committed murder is that they have witnessed or were victims of domestic violence. I remember as a child watching my father violently abuse my older sister. She had to spend days in a hospital afterwards. I remember my father angrily pushing my head through a small window in a door in our home and later helping my mom pull pieces of glass out of my head. My mother would put us to bed in our clothes and then sneak us out of a window to hide in bushes at 1, 2, 3:00 a.m. for fear of what my father might do as he would come home drunk. But these (and many other acts of violence we witnessed in the home) incidents were never mentioned, healed or discussed and reconciliation never took place. These personal examples of domestic violence incidents unfortunately are not uncommon in many American homes. Yet, kids who grow up like this are expected to get up, go to school on time, be good, sit still, listen, and concentrate on the given lesson, which are often times explained in a language or vocabulary over their heads, let alone their emotions. But when kids are not doing well in school, have a short attention span, show signs of depression or act out in defiant ways; we are quick to label them with learning disorders, intellectual inferiority or other negative social labels. While I recognize that there are some children who have learning disabilities, I cannot help but wonder how many are the result of unresolved emotional trauma?

I'll never forget the cold, dead, empty tearless heart I felt as an 18 year old looking down into the casket of my father. At that moment I just didn't care or feel any sense of loss or regret. The point is, these are inward issues that an "outside-in" (as I call it) – after school or community program approach is usually not going to address, yet they are preventing so many kids from reaching their potential. However, I am happy to testify to the scores of young people I have seen turn their grades, as well as their life, around because of an "inside-out" personal approach that turned a heart full of anxiety and anger to one of forgiving, healing, resolve and peace.

Listen to part of this young man's story from a letter he sent to me back in 1998 describing his experience with the inside-out transformation I am referring to:

> *Dear Richard...I just wanted to take the time to express my appreciation and gratitude. I just received my computer last week. For as long as I could remember, the church has always been my adopted family. I still remember the love and affection upon my first visit to the church...at the time I was suicidal, involved with gangs, drugs, alcohol, I was constantly running away, I was full of confusion, doubt, anger, and hatred and I had lost all hope and respect for everything in my life. At the time Ronnie had become my closest friend. He took me under his wing and became the father I never had. He put up with me for years...Meanwhile, the church was providing me with things I felt I had never experienced, like acceptance and unconditional love...I'm now at UC Berkley, one of the*

top Universities in the world, and I know the church family had a big role in that...I have so many people that I see as father and mother figures and I've never taken this for granted. I just wanted to thank everybody..."
- Cesar Perfecto

Today this young man is a proud graduate from UC Berkeley and working with at-risk youth in his community, giving back and repeating the process of reaching similar "angry hearts" with the inside-out approach of personal transformation. This inside-out transformation occurs when a child's heart experiences this "healing and emptying of anger". This provides room for an infilling of peace and joy that liberates them to learn and grow. It is no longer full and preoccupied with physical and emotional survival and has new space to receive other positive influences. The question is how do you turn a violent and angry heart into one of peace and joy?

Hood understood = transformation

What I have found with gang members is the loss of their individual self-worth. Many lost their childhood and innocence at such an early age that they have no concept of who they really are and who they can truly become. If we are ignorant to this, or insensitive to them, we will miss many opportunities to effectively intervene in the lives of these kids. We can help turn them around when that little opening in their heart occurs and is inviting us into their private, real self. This is what is meant by the phrase; *Hood understood equals transformation.* The following three stories illustrate that we can effectively intervene through properly exercising our authority, make unpopular decisions, and still be instruments of transformation.

El Vato Loco

I recall a conversation I had one day with a gang member who showed up at my teen center with his brother and "homies". They were high on alcohol, drugs or both so they came up acting loud and rowdy as usual. One of them was particularly high and acting what we would call "stupid", i.e. embarrassing himself and his homeboys. I got up out of my chair to go outside and see if the staff member (a woman) had things under control, which she did, as she was familiar with the kid acting "crazy". I noticed that the kid standing in front of me had a broken stick in his hand with a sharp pointy end and was holding it down on his side so as to conceal it from my sight. He went around me into the office and wanted to use the phone. I followed him and told him he couldn't come in with the stick and tried to grab it from him. But he didn't let me and in a loud, sarcastic voice, told me not to touch it, as it was his cane he was using to walk with as he had hurt his leg. I then told him he had to leave my office and needed to change his attitude and tone of voice if he wanted to stay. At this point we were face to face. I wasn't trying to be hard, or get rid of them, and I knew he could sense that in me. In my mind, it was just another opportunity to teach, influence and establish the form of respect that is required with gang members. Luckily for both of us, he backed down and went outside. Had he not, I honestly don't know what I would have done, other than the obvious, which was to get physical, a very bad, unpredictable situation one should try to avoid at all costs.

A few moments later, after this little "confrontation", the young man returned not only to apologize, but also to open up about his life and his desire to change the struggle he was having. As I began to listen and encourage him, tears welled up in his eyes and these were his words;

> *"It is so hard for me to be around people who have had a mom and a dad, a nice life...I can't relate to them and I feel weird around them.... Most kids at my age (18) just begin to experience drugs like weed or alcohol...since the time I was 7 or 8 I have been around heroin, cocaine... and my mom used to use me to take it into prisons.... You just don't know what I have seen and been around and it is just hard to change..."*

This is what I continually find with gang members. The names and times are different of course but the situations and circumstances are almost always the same. There always seems to come a time, at different points in their lives, when they get tired, want to change, and put down all their fronts of acting hard, mean and tough. The little kid inside of them is crying out for love, attention, acceptance and the freedom and safety to express their real self. This may not sound scientific, but it is the best way to describe what I have witnessed over and over again as a father and person in authority that has helped in the transformation of so many gang members. After our talk we were able to establish a relationship and our program was able to help this young man.

Christina

The second story of this "Hood understood = transformation" phenomenon is about a young Latina girl I will call Christina. I knew that one day she would come to me about her life and education. I did not know when, but I did know why. She, like so many other gang members I have counseled over the years, was living in the same type of environment and making the same destructive choices that I have witnessed too many times before. Eventually (as in the first story), most come to the point where they get tired of *la vida loca (the crazy life),* and begin to look outside "their world" for answers to a change of lifestyle.

I first met Christina when she was fourteen years old. She was caught up in boys, drugs, and the gang sub-culture, bent on being mean and building a reputation of beating up any girl that would challenge her in one way or another. My initial experience with her was typical. She was rude, disrespectful, short, and just plain mean with me, as I was the "new boss on the block" that had stepped into her turf and I had to earn her respect, etc. It is always that way, yet I knew the other, long-term side of it also, and treated her with the same kindness, dignity, and humility, yet firm authority, with which I have always treated gang members in order to build a respectful and trusting relationship that will eventually allow me to have influence in their lives.

Four years later (and after eating a lot of humble pie, just to keep the door of relationship open with her that I knew she would eventually need), she walked into my office one night "out of nowhere". I had not seen her for a while, as to this point, she rarely came to the teen center. As she came into my office and sat down, unannounced, I could see that look on her face that I have seen in so many other young faces of gang members over the years. Privately, she began to share with me that she was *tired*. Although I knew exactly what she meant and where "we" were going, I asked her what she meant, to give her what she desperately needed, *the opportunity to be heard and understood without lecture or judgment.* Christina was the typical Latina student who possessed all the ability necessary to succeed in school, but had chosen rather to act up in class, ditch, etc. and was eventually placed in the County Alternative classroom, where she was not doing well.

To get to the point I am making here, she eventually began to cry, tell me how much she hated being disliked and feared by people. Her heart was broken because her teachers and administrators where telling her to just *move on and not waste her time*. She was also tired of all the "drama" at home, and was sad that some of her friends had "gotten it together" and were flaunting the fact that they were going to graduate and she wasn't. Amidst her tears and sobbing, I said, *"Christina what is it that you really want? Tell me, what do you want?* She looked up at me, and with a serious and tearful face said, *"I want to earn my diploma and graduate from high school."*

This is the point at which there is a break down and separation of opinions of what should be done in cases like this. This is where so many parents, teachers and administrators give the *"well, you should of, could of, and would of speech"* and kindly patronize these kids into discouragement, which leads them to giving up and dropping out. This is exactly where Christina found herself, yet I saw it as a window of opportunity to get her back into her studies and working toward her diploma.

The tragedy, in these transforming moments, is that gang members often have no one to turn to that will listen, understand, and provide them with answers, time and the example of how to complete the transformation. Too often their plea for help falls on deaf, un-empathetic ears. The message of intervention is; kids want to change, can change and it is never, never, too late! The message to parents is; who better for our kids to go to in these transforming moments than their own mother and father?

Jimmy

This leads me to the third story to further illustrate the *Hood understood* concept and its effectiveness in taking the time to understand gang members and to treat them with respect, yet at the same time not allowing them to bully you or intimidate you into disregarding their disrespectful and disobedient behavior.

I will call him Jimmy. When I first arrived at the teen center he was unquestionably the worst kid we had. He was very angry, very defiant, and refusing to take any instruction or discipline from anyone. He was frequently being "kicked out" or suspended for a few days, and would leave cursing and throwing things at the building, etc. I knew this angry out burst of behavior meant a few things, but one thing in particular, I knew this was a kid with deep "heart" pain caused by unresolved injustices of some kind in his personal life. This is what I know in general, but the specifics vary from one kid to another.

As I observed Jimmy over a few months time and made my deposits of love, respect, and kindness to him, (along with times of firm but quiet confrontations) I suggested a call be made to his home to possibly talk to his mother just to get a feel for what was going on at home. To my knowledge this had not yet been done. This is a very important point. Often times those who provide gang intervention services neglect to involve the parents. This is a mistake in most cases. We tend to view a teen and his behavior apart from his/her family, instead of from within their family, which almost always gives a much better understanding and perspective of the person. What we discovered upon speaking to his mother was not a surprise to me. However, it was certainly insightful and allowed us to have much more patience, compassion, and understanding for this boy. What we discovered was when Jimmy was about 9 or 10 years old (he was 13 when I met him) he witnessed his father commit suicide and had never discussed it or dealt with it in any way. Neither he nor his mother had ever discussed it or dealt with it and never received help after the initial incident. The mother went on to say that we (teen center) were the first people she really had a chance to talk to about it in any length. Following this, Jimmy's mother visited the teen center regularly to talk. We eventually referred her to a family service agency who could help her further. Since this took place, we have seen a remarkable turn around in this young man. He smiles much more, is much easier to talk to and learning how to respect others, which leads me to the success story I began to share.

Jimmy was eating an orange and sitting on a couch in the teen center with his friends. Without thinking anything about it, he and his friend threw their peelings on the floor. One of the new employees gave them a command to pick up their orange peelings to which they began to protest against. In the past, there is no way this young man would have obeyed. He would rather have been kicked out than to listen to anybody tell him what he could and could not do. As I sat in the office nearby I heard this exchange going on in the constant battle for respect, obedience and control between staff members and teenage gang members. I decided I'd better help so I stuck my head out of the door, called his name, and simply gave him a look of "…come on man, what's the problem? Just do it!" (Yes it is possible to communicate all that with one look) and lo and behold, he did!!! I remember having such a sense of pride in him, accomplishment, satisfaction, and joy!! For this young man this was such a step of personal growth.

Not long after this incident, Jimmy came to visit and talk to me at the teen center. He looked good. He came to ask if I would help him by writing a letter of character for him. This is something I have had the opportunity to do for so many kids who have come back to me later. As was the case in all three stories. They disliked me at first, as I am someone who stands up to them, challenges their intimidation and calls them into accountability. Yet, because I balance this with love, respect, flexibility and fairness, over time, they learn to understand me, respect me and befriend me as a father figure to them.

I believe these stories are typical of so many other gang members, who want to and would change their defiant behavior if someone would just take the time to listen to them and help them express their hearts in a safe environment. I know this is true because it happened with me and with so many others that I have had the privilege of working with over the years like the young man in the story below:

> *"My mother took a brave step by leaving my father, (who was an abusive alcoholic), when I was just a toddler. She raised us during the sixties and seventies while she was a university student...I remember feeling lonely at an early age. Depressed, anxious, without hope, I was acting weird enough that she took me to a psychiatrist who probed me with endless questions and evaluations...Dad never tried to support or contact us. So mom did what she could to feed and clothe us. One year we lived in a converted chicken coup with no electricity, no plumbing or heating and no windows. Mom worked and we went to school. At night, mom cooked and we warmed ourselves at the small camping burner next to her bed. Later, we upgraded to*

the overcrowded, huge housing projects, which were full of crime and violence.

I filled the role of a neighborhood menace: a "Cholo". I proudly strolled down the streets as one of many home-boys. I sported crisp khaki pants a nice Pendleton shirt, my hair combed back in a sharp blue bandana. I "belonged" in the gang-crowds of young Chicanos gathering at parks, drinking in the dark streets and in garage parties of the neighborhood. We listened to "oldies" and got high any way we could. We cruised in custom cars with the older veterano's who got us high and taught us the code. We stole bikes, robbed cars and burglarized houses. It was easy to wear this brand since my skin was brown and acceptance was almost automatic. All one needed to do was get credibility, know the game, the players and step up to challengers...What are you gonna do in a community where the lines between weak and strong are clearly marked? Besides, I enjoyed the night life and being on the giving side of intimidation.

I was kicked out of high school 6 months into 9th grade. I was sent to a special school for troubled kids "in the system", but never finished the program. By 10th grade, friends were dying and the parties we crashed were remembered more for their stabbings, gunshots and crowded street fights, than their original purpose...My identity was wrapped up in this lifestyle—-easy to learn, harder to live as time went on.

I spent summers with my father who prided himself on drinking and fighting. To dad, "manhood" meant taking me into the bars drinking with him till the early morning hours...On the streets he was violent and obnoxious and I tried to emulate him. Joining in on his drunken stupors, I'd fight our way out of the bars and even pick fights with his trouble making buddies in the bars. After a brief time spent in the military, I plunged right back into alcohol and drugs: Acid, mushrooms, marijuana, speed, codeine and heroin. I took everything I got my hands on. In a short time, I was injecting cocaine. Any loyalties I'd known in the past—ended. At the age of 20, I was bankrupt, emotionally, physically, financially and spiritually —- no job, no home, no real friends, even family had seen enough. The chip on my shoulder had been ground down by life!

I learned about Richard Ramos when I met a stranger, a former gang-member who stopped me on the street and invited me to a church service...The church was full of young people like me with similar backgrounds, now living productive, clean, purposeful lives...I was encouraged to discover my unique gifts, and talents through opportunities provided... including, teaching, administration, outreach to youth and leadership development. These helped me later in community work and business.

Christina and I were married in 1988: Our children grew from toddlers to teens and adults. Our marriage and parenting were strengthened by the Parents on a Mission

classes taught by Richard. In particular, I learned that the greatest security my children would experience is seeing that my wife and I share a love and dedication for each other and for God...Since having my three children...I've finished High School, & College. I started a career as an Insurance Professional. I built up, owned and sold a successful Insurance business. I now have a career in Real Estate and Finance. I am prosperous both materially and personally in ways I never dreamed possible. Today I'm blessed and fulfilled as a husband and a father.
–Joe Garnica

Nobody wants to "be bad". Nobody likes "being bad". It goes against our conscience even if we don't understand it.

CHAPTER 12

Consequences of disrespect for parental authority

"Many a spoiled child is the kind of youngster
his mother tells him not to play with"
– Anonymous

I realize the challenge many parents face both in establishing their authority and regaining lost authority. Nevertheless, when searching for answers to the bigger social problems parents face in raising their kids in today's American culture, I still believe that much of the problems with our youth stem back to this issue of a lack of respect for authority. This forces others in the community to deal with this rebellious attitude in a variety of settings outside the home, the consequences of which are sometimes much more severe than inside the home.

As an example of the importance of this, allow me to share some additional experiences I had as the director of the teen center mentioned before. We had numerous incidents, problems, dilemmas and situations which presented many challenges to our staff, students and parents, which all speak to the point of the importance of parental authority. My staff and I tried a number of different approaches to solve the following list of on-going problems we faced with gang members attending the center on a regular basis:

A List of Challenges

1. What is the most effective way of working with gang members in their own neighborhood?

2. How do you establish control and authority that is respected, without losing their interest in your program?

3. How do you, or can you, mix a gang culture with non-gang youth?

4. How do you motivate unmotivated students to take advantage of a tutoring program?

5. What is the best way to deal with young men who are verbally harassing female students and staff?

6. What measures should be taken when staff members are threatened with bodily harm when enforcing rules against drinking, drug use, smoking, stealing, etc.?

7. What measures should be taken when staff members' property is vandalized as a direct result of enforcing policies and rules?

8. What measures should be taken to bring consequences for members who break into a staff member's home to steal, party, and vandalize personal property?

9. What consequences, if any, should a center impose upon members who commit acts of violence against other community members?

10. What is the best way to stop members from "tagging" on their own center?

11. How should the staff respond when gang members "jump" other kids who are members of the same center?

12. What is the most effective way of controlling the constant use of profanity with no regard for staff?

13. What forms of discipline, punishment and consequences are best for youth who have little fear of consequences, no respect for rules, reject authority, have no regard for the welfare of others, and no care for valuable property and resources?

14. How do you deal with parents who refuse to accept responsibility for the negative behavior of their children, yet still want ownership and authority in the programs?

In my view, one of the first actions to be taken with such rebellious, defiant and violent behavior is to contact the parents of these individuals and let them handle their own kids' behavior. However, as you read item number 14 on the list, you will notice that we tried that approach and many of the parents were unwilling to admit that their kids were that bad, the classic case of being in denial. Another immediate reaction is to simply remove the kids from the program. Well that would be defeating the very purpose and reason for the existence of the program to reach these youth gang members in the barrio. Thus, there are no easy answers or quick fixes to any of these problems. Yet, they are the realities with which many schools and youth programs deal with on a daily basis. And whether one thinks you know what to do, or not, you are forced to make decisions regarding these and other complicated issues which your target audience bring with them to the program.

At this point we can see at least two core issues. One is, in most cases, kids raised in a home where they have been taught to respect their parent's authority don't normally cause these types of public problems.

Secondly, a decision of where to place our time and resources to provide solutions to these problems needs to be made. The answer of course is to place time and resources into both kids and their parents, and (as mentioned earlier) stop investing the majority of government funding in law enforcement suppression.

This also raises the point of recognizing the limitations of the "whole village" concept in raising children. I understand the good intentions behind this concept, but I just think it was spoken for another time in our nation's past, and has become obsolete as a barrio strategy, especially with all the child kidnappings, teacher-student molestations and murders taking place on a regular basis. It also places too much emphasis on the answer to raising healthy and respectful kids as the responsibility of society rather than individual parents. Again, I am not suggesting that parents don't need or want help with their kids, but based on what I have described above as the daily experience we had at our teen center, many of these problems could have been resolved had there been solid parental authority to appeal to. As a "village" we were limited in what we could do and were forced to ask many of the kids to leave and not return if they refused to obey and respect the rules. This was not the solution we wanted to use, but without the parental authority to rely on, we were forced to resort to that as an answer and the kids, parents and community all end up losers because we lose the potential in each of those rejected from the program simply because they could not, or would not accept, respect and obey authority. As the reader might have assumed, many of the gang members who chose not to comply and left the program, were eventually incarcerated.

CHAPTER 13

Reestablishing authority for parents & teachers

"A real leader faces the music when he doesn't like the tune"
– A. Glassgow

Reestablishing one's authority is difficult work whether a parent or teacher dealing with kids with intervention needs. It is a kind of daily struggle that is emotionally and psychologically draining. Working to reestablish the acceptance of one's authority is a slow process and it is very possible that we will not see the positive effect we may have had on an individual. To endure in the service of a gang intervention specialist takes a "farmer's heart". "Community farmers" (as I call them) are planters of seeds, cultivators of fertile soil, and are constantly watering these young souls. If we stay with it long enough, we may be able to actually harvest our own seed that we have "farmed" for years. I've been fortunate to reap some of my own fruit and the rewards of this are great and very satisfying. To actually witness the transformation of a rebellious/defiant gang member ("reaping what you have sowed") is probably one of the biggest sources of inspiration that parents and teachers can derive from working with "bad kids". Thus, reestablishing your authority is not always pleasant or popular at the time, nonetheless it is good and right to roll up your sleeves and be that "farmer". I can promise you, if you do the work needed, you will one day get to enjoy your own fruit.

Going the second mile as a parent and teacher reminds us of why we are in this work to begin with, which is that we possess some measure of hope for all kids. We believe that every kid wants to be good and inherently has the capacity to be good. We believe that whatever wrongs or problems have caused their hearts to be turned to bad behavior and habits, are internal issues that can be undone through the persistence of a relationship of trust, modeling, discipline, fairness and unconditional love.

The majority of people who become parents or go into teaching do not desire to be an authority figure. Their first thought in having children or working with children was not to become an authority figure, exercise discipline, enforce rules, or shape character. The first, natural inclination is simply to have a family, or in the case of the teacher, is to be "cool", accepted, and liked by kids. To be liked is a very necessary part of the job, but this is not all that is required if you want to be respected by kids who need intervention. What you will soon come to realize is that the kids will "like" you as long as you never say "no" to them. If you let them do whatever they want, then you will be "cool", but they will mock you if you ever try to get them to obey you on your terms. They will never take your authority serious because you have opted to be "liked", over being effective in earning respect and control. It is possible to have both, but it takes a lot of emotional maturity, consistency and fair but firm enforcement of the rules.

To accomplish this, it is not necessary to be harsh, mean, unapproachable or disrespectful. It is necessary to be unpopular at times, to reestablish "who is in control around here", i.e., respect for your authority. This is vital to anyone interested in truly helping these kids out of their selfish, rebellious and immature character which is the cause of most of their problems with authority at home, in school, and at work. It is easy to be "cool", but to shape character, build integrity, and cultivate maturity and tame rebelliousness is usually not cool or easy. Yet, it is necessary. On the other hand, it is easy to be abusive in the use of authority as a means of control. However, the real work is learning to be skillful in shaping character without shaming, belittling, or being intimidated out of correctly exerting authority when it calls for it. Anyone can show self-control, calmness, patience, and kindness when there is no pressure. What marks the effective parents and teachers are those who demonstrate these virtues of character and maturity when facing stressful and unexpected difficult circumstances. This will not happen without training and the consistent practice of the principles of building healthy human relationships in one's real life situations.

CHAPTER 14

The proper use of authority

"Submit to the rule you laid down"
– English proverb

Reaction is usually negative and requires no thought. It is like the instinctive nature of animals, which are not endowed with the ability of reasoning and taking a moment to "think about their thinking". All they have to rely on is their reactionary instincts to outside stimulus. Human beings are not limited to basic instincts. It is imperative that authority figures both understand this, and develop their capacity to choose a response that will help a situation, rather than to make it worse. This takes instruction and practice but is very effective when learned and applied with gang members.

Our inclination as parents and authority figures in a tough, tense and troubled situation is to *"borrow from our strength"* most of the time. What this phrase means is that we play our trump card of authority by kicking them out, or we use our physical strength, our louder voice, our knowledge, or whatever "strength" we possess that will resolve the situation most efficiently in our favor. However, being *efficient* does not always guarantee *effectiveness,* which is most important when dealing with intervention and striving to develop transforming relationships on a regular basis.

This, of course, begs the question, "what is a right or effective response?" In the "El Vato Loco" story I shared it would have been easy, and within our policy, to make the youth leave the grounds immediately because they were high on drugs and alcohol. I could have even called the nearby Sheriff's foot patrol because of the stick, that could have easily been perceived as a weapon to cause others physical harm and would have been grounds to have the youth arrested. However, if I had "reacted" that way, I would have missed the transforming opportunity that came later.

More often than not, I have witnessed parents and public authority figures react in a wrong way to wrong youth behavior. In one of my classes to parents I'd say, *"when our kid's do the wrong thing, we need to do the right thing."* This means we need to practice our ability to pause and think of our response. It means that we realize that preaching or giving a lecture may not be the best response at the moment. Maybe silence and listening is called for, or a supportive hug to let them know that we will work this out together. It means we stop ourselves from resorting to the easy reaction of using belittling names, punishing them, putting them down or embarrassing them in front of other people. Sometimes, the right thing to do with wrong behavior is to respond with patience, understanding and flexibility. Having said that, each case, whether at home or in public depends on the circumstances leading up to the situation. While it is a bit different for parents than it would be for a teacher, some of the following guidelines apply for both.

a. The "right response" will require knowledge of the history of the individual(s) involved, the history of your interaction with the individual(s), an understanding of the bigger picture and long-term impacts of your decision.

b. It also depends on who is witnessing your response, where the situation is taking place, and how many are involved.

c. As a teacher, it may be that you have no background information and it is the first time you are dealing with the individual (as was the case in my first story), in which case, a different response would be called for as opposed to one from a teacher familiar with the history of the individual (as was the case in my second story).

d. This kind of "response" usually must be decided upon in a matter of seconds, which is why training and practice is so important.

e. This does not mean that those in authority can, or are expected to always have the right response, or that the right response will necessarily "fix" the problem at hand. However, I do suggest that if those in authority would be trained in how to make this type of mature, parental/professional effort when faced with these situations, it would solve many more problems, rather than the usual negative reaction, or passive non-reaction that perpetuates them. It would also serve as a positive model for teens of the proper use of authority.

f. If we are to be effective with this, and the next generation of youth, we need to work to re-establish the foundation of authority and re-define authority as a "friend," rather than an "enemy" to be despised.

g. True authority does not come with simply being placed in a position of authority.

h. True authority is earned from a relationship of trust, built on the integrity of your word and the example of your lifestyle.

i. True authority is measured by one's scope of influence, not by one's position as a parent, social status, salary, material wealth, elected office or professional promotions.

j. Ultimately, true authority has to do with whether or not our children choose to obey and follow us, not out of fear, but out of love, respect and trust.

In working with Latino youth and in particular with gang members, I have witnessed the difference the respect for authority makes in a learning environment. Let me explain:

For some reason, Latino kids love "capping" (Latino slang for making fun of someone), especially in a learning or serious situation. I am not sure why this is, and I have been guilty of it myself many times to the point of being kicked out of the classroom because I could not stop laughing as I was "capping" on a friend, the teacher or both. This can really get out of hand in a classroom and if the teacher has no respect, or no authority, it becomes a frustrating game of "cat and mouse" almost on a daily basis and consequently little productivity is achieved in such an environment. On the surface it seems funny and not a big deal. However, youth can be brutal in the comments they make and they don't realize the impact they have on an individual's self-esteem, social status among peers and their personal motivation to learn and excel academically. It seems that there exists a real fear by peers to lose friends to success, or to be left out, or behind, by friends who begin to show loyalty to education ("being a school girl/boy"; i.e. "smart"). Thus, they begin to try and pull down, or keep down, their friends who begin to climb out of, grow out of, and break out of the Latino neighborhood "brown ceiling".

In order to encourage this "breaking out", young people must feel safe if they are to truly develop their potential as human beings. They must be exposed to an environment free of ridicule, shame, criticism and judgment. They must have constant and consistent cultivation in an atmosphere of encouragement, tolerance, appreciation and unconditional love. They must be challenged to strive to new heights, learning not to be hampered by the fear of failure. They must learn the pathway to self-knowledge, which is the key to achieving personal excellence. I suggest that developing such an environment in a place like a public classroom is nearly impossible without the proper use of authority.

PART II

GANG-BANGER IN THE CLASSROOM

CHAPTER 15

Seven principles for helping Gang members become productive students

"What and how much responsibility do teachers play preventing gang involvement? Is it a teacher's job to try to prevent involvement, and if so, what do you think would be an effective teaching strategy in order to do that"?
– Kelly, Classroom teacher

Dear Kelly,
Teachers play an important role in this area. Teachers are responsible for the youth while he or she is in their care or control. The fact is that at times teachers tend to see the different changes a kid goes through before the parents do. Taking all these factors under account, how can a teacher not get involved when they see a student going down the wrong path, which will undermine all that the teacher is teaching the youth?

Is it the teacher's job to try to prevent their involvement? This is a very difficult question. I do not really believe that you can consider this "a teacher's job" to stop a kids involvement into a gang. However, how can a person call themselves a teacher if they see a kid going down the path of destruction and yet do nothing. No, it is not a teacher's job to do this but a teacher should take it upon himself and/or go out of their way to make sure they do not lose a kid to the streets or to gangs. But how far is a person willing to go? And should that teacher put himself/herself in danger or harms' way to insure? I say no, they should not. The best strategy is for teachers and parents to work together to form a partnership where during the times that the youth is under the supervision of the teacher, the teacher is the eyes and ears of the parents. The youth should also be part of this partnership so they will not develop any ill feelings between the youth and the teacher, for those times when the teacher has to speak to the parents, the youth do not feel like the teacher is "ratting" him or her out. This is also important so the teacher can get to know the family of his or her students. Knowing the family will better prepare the teacher to deal with the behavior of the youth. Together I am sure the teacher and the parents can come up with a positive alternative to gang life and be able to constantly reinforce the family values needed to insure the youth's good future. Sincerely - Luis D.

Dear Kelly,

I truly believe that teachers play a strong role in our kid's lives. It's not a teacher's responsibility to prevent their involvement. What parents wouldn't want help to prevent their kids from joining gangs. A strategy for teachers to help our children is to treat them as if they are their own. It is helpful to build a relationship with them.

Sincerely, Michael R.

Teachers play a secondary role in the socialization process of our children. The primary responsibility rests with the family. However, because teachers are involved, they have the responsibility of educating our youth on citizenship (the status of a citizen with its attendant duties, rights and responsibilities). Many of our schools have gotten away from teaching this kind of curriculum. They've allowed the influences of the 60's and 70's to dictate that if it's not reading, writing and arithmetic; it shouldn't be taught in our schools. No, I'm not advocating the introduction of prayer and religion in our schools. That's an area that is better suited to a parent's responsibility. Morality, on the other hand, is a subject matter that teachers could easily teach our children. To help a parent by teaching our youth about being in accord with the standards of right or good conduct is something a teacher should aspire to.

–Angel C.

(Above question and answers by prison inmates from: www.gangsandkids.com)

Before we move on to the seven principles, please indulge me as I give some context and explain a few things to the teachers I am offering these principles to. I have the utmost respect and appreciation for those who are daily in the classrooms of our schools. In many cases, the classroom teacher is among the unsung hero's of the community; often going beyond the call of duty in their dedication to the kids they interact with daily. While the purpose of this portion of the book is to offer teachers insight, guidelines and understanding, particularly with gang members, I am well aware that most of the teachers in our public schools are excellent people and this portion of the book is in no way intended to be a negative criticism of all teachers. Yet, I do believe there is a need to address the issue of gang members in the classroom for three reasons. First, gang members do exist in our schools and this has caused some particular problems. Second, we are losing too many youth to *alternative classroom education,* and too many of those who are placed in alternative schools are Latino and often-considered gang members or gang affiliated. Third, in most cases, gang members are misunderstood, and there seems to be a negative over emphasis on these "kinds of kids" who become the target of some teachers, principles, and school districts that too easily dismiss them, mishandle them, and discourage their participation on campus. Consequently, many become discouraged, begin to ditch class, or drop out, thus making them prime candidates for probation and the juvenile justice system. I suggest that part of the reason these, and many other similar situations, happen as frequently as they do is because of a lack of communication, misunderstanding, a lack of knowledge, and cultural insensitivity on the part of some public school officials.

I am not advocating for these kids to be given a "free ride", or to exempt them from accepting the responsibility of the bad choices they have made along the way, etc. I am simply saying that it seems there is not the same level of communication, understanding, tolerance and willingness to make extra efforts, and in some cases exceptions for these kids, as there is for others. Because of the many diverse challenges today's Latino students present to classroom teachers, it seems that what was needed to train teachers of the past, is no longer sufficient for what is needed in the classrooms of today and tomorrow. Today's students present issues that are the same "in kind", but not "in degree". Language barriers, cultural preferences, social and domestic pressures, lack of motivation, cynicism, lack of trust, little respect for authority, and a host of other issues, may sound like the *same old problems,* but, in my judgment, they have increased with a degree in which teachers of the past did not face. These issues need to be understood from *their perspective,* and this requires specialized training. For example, athletes need more than just good teaching. They also require good coaching, which is an important distinction to make from teaching. While teaching requires the ability to communicate knowledge, *coaching* takes teaching a step further that elevates the player to a higher level of competition. Not all good teachers are good coaches, but all good coaches are good teachers. I suggest, in working with gang members in the classroom, that one step in helping good teachers to become good coaches is to give them more understanding of the gang member mentality, or paradigm, which this section of the book attempts to offer.

The material of these seven principles is based on my own personal experience as a Chicano/American-Mexican student in the sixties and seventies. Additionally, my experiences are also based on what I have witnessed working as a correctional officer at a State and Federal prison, as well as being a teachers aide in the Santa Barbara County Juvenile Hall for four years. In addition to running the teen center, I was an "at-risk" counselor for four years at a local junior high and high school

(1990-94), where I worked directly with the school administration, teachers, counselors, probation, law enforcement and parents of gang members. Although these insights may seem challenging to teachers, they are offered respectfully and in a spirit of cooperation. These seven principles are certainly not exhaustive or scientific, but they have worked for me as I have already described earlier in the book. In any case, I share them for the classroom teacher, who has a true desire to deal with gang members who are causing them problems. I believe there are many such teachers who sincerely want to reach out to these students, but simply don't know how, or where to begin. As problems persist, they are forced to remove the student and lose them to a system they know is not to their benefit. I am convinced that these teachers wonder to themselves how they can make a difference in these kids and help turn them from becoming another negative Latino student statistic.

Finally, I must point out that my suggestions are not a guarantee for fixing every situation described, nor am I emphasizing my particular practices, but rather the principle, of handling difficult people problems. With that, I offer these seven insights that have helped my work in successfully transforming many Latino gang members into productive students and citizens of their community.

PRINCIPLE 1 – HUMILITY

Humility leads to strength and not to weakness. It is the highest form of self-respect to admit mistakes and to make amends for them.
–John J. McCloy

The mistake of "fronting off" is one of the most common mistakes teachers make with gang members. "Fronting off", means to belittle, embarrass, command or challenge a student *in front* of their friends. It usually is prompted by some type of disobedience, disruption, or defiance by the student, that is "fronting off" the teacher. There are usually plenty of daily opportunities for a student to "front off" a teacher, and for a teacher to "front off" a student, but the wise teacher refrains from using this as a technique for gaining control over a situation. Most teachers probably don't purposely *front off,* or realize what they have done, while others may simply not care. Others care, but lack the self-control to avoid making this mistake, once they have been *fronted off,* and embarrassed themselves. Two simple lessons to be learned to help avoid the "fronting off" battle are:

1. Correction without relationship breed's rebellion.
2. Meet the students' demand for public respect first, and then privately earn yours.

Some simple examples of how the above two lessons present themselves as opportunities are:

- When a student comes in the classroom late, talking loud, and disrupts the teacher.
- When a student is talking to friends, etc., and the teacher is trying to give instruction.
- A student who is doing nothing, and the teacher decides to point them out in front of the whole class and commands them to do something.

These three examples provide the teacher with an opportunity for a relationship that could very well cause this student to become very productive in their classroom if the teacher is willing to exercise or acquire some basic skills in tactical maneuvering of building relationships. When the student fronts off the teacher, it is very important for the teacher to assess the situation and quickly think about the proper response, since the whole class is usually watching. This takes practice, but can be a learned response over time. In too many cases, the teacher gives in to the easy, reactive behavior, of saying something loud, negative and embarrassing to the student. This technique may work sometimes, with some kids. But for the most part, the teacher has now contributed to a problem that could go on and on, which inevitably ends up in the teachers' favor, by a win/lose solution of getting rid of the problem/student, rather than, working to find a win/win solution.

As one 22-year-old L.A. gang member put it; *"The schools weren't teaching me anything. The teachers just saw me as a trouble maker, and their prejudices kept them from seeing if I had any potential at all."*

Even if the kid submits at that moment, the problem will most likely continue. The student will usually retaliate at some point during the remainder of the class or the next day. Why? Because they must "save face" and maintain their status and respect with their friends. They know their friends will "cap" (Latino slang for make fun of) on them after class, after school, and in the neighborhood. The more "capping" one receives, the more they are under pressure to retaliate to prove that they are not going to let the teacher "front them off", or "punk them" (slang for making somebody look weak; sissy, etc.) like that again! Otherwise, they become someone considered "weak" that can be picked on by others with no "pay-back". This is especially true among gang members.

In most cases, like the ones described above, the best thing to do is nothing, at that moment, if at all possible. The wise thing is to wait until you can deal with the student one-on-one, in private, and begin to try to build a relationship. I realize this may, or may not be possible, as each of these types of incidents are judgment calls by the teacher, based on a variety of factors. These include: the history of the individual(s) involved, the history of your interaction with the individual(s), an understanding of the bigger picture and long-term impacts of your decision. It also depends on who is witnessing your response, what time during the class the incident takes place, and how many are involved. It may be that you have no background or experience with the student, and it is the first time you are dealing with him or her, in which case, a different response would be called for. I am not suggesting that the teacher can, or is expected to, always have the correct response, or that the right response will necessarily "fix" the problem at the moment. However, I do suggest that if the teacher makes the choice to exercise the principle of humility, it would solve many more problems, rather than the usual negative reaction that perpetuates them. It would also serve as a positive model for the other students in how to professionally handle a difficult situation. Your ego will be bruised a little, but I have found that a humble response, in the long run, has gained me much more favor with the difficult student, as well as, the rest of the class.

One key in this strategy is that the student understands they have done wrong, and using this approach, in most cases, will drive that conviction even deeper. They also know that your courteous and respectful way of handling them was right, and allowed them to "save face", which goes a long way, with gang members in particular. Your non-action wins respect because you chose to give it, instead of demand it, in front of the other students. Deciding not to *front them off* has now put them in your debt, which is something they understand and will want to pay off. They will usually pay back the favor with classroom cooperation, after you deal with them privately, and may get others to follow, as often times, the one doing the "clowning" is the leader amongst their peers. If the teacher can win the respect and trust of the leader, it will go a long way in creating a productive learning environment, as "the power of one" principle suggests that the one influences the many and the teacher will have tapped into this. I suggest that choosing the response of humility, when fronted off is one way of achieving these results.

I have personally witnessed the power of this principle over and over again throughout my many years of working with gang members, whose potential is often buried in shame, pride, anger and a street culture that does not value American education. If teachers, who get fronted off can look past the outward behavior, and focus on trying to build a respectful relationship, they could help turn around many problem students.
The following is an excerpt from one of my trainings, sharing my personal experience in exercising the principle of humility and my reason-

ing behind it, as a new director of a teen center:

> *The first thing we need to be effective with these kids, is trust. This can only come after time spent with them in genuine caring and involvement in their personal pain. They need to know that they are safe around you to be who they are without judgment or lecturing, and moralizing. They have the same needs we all have which is to simply be accepted for who they are right now. It doesn't mean we agree or have to leave them that way. Those things can be addressed later.*
>
> *Once I spent time establishing my heart with theirs, I knew the next step would be to confront them in a kind, respectful, but firm way. In this case I did not spend as long a time depositing my heart into them to establish trust, as I normally would have. This assessment of timing had to do with a few factors. One was the program that we were operating, called for an environment conducive to studying and tutoring. Another had to do with the smallness of the building which we all had to share as multiple activities were going on at the same time. The other factor had to do with the diversity of age ranges and the bad example that was being set and followed by the younger kids.*
>
> *In establishing respect and authority, timing is important, but it is not going to be the same in every case. If you exert it too soon you will make it harder to establish. Waiting too long makes it harder to undo the norms that*

have been set by the kids, and more kids are influenced by a negative lifestyle in social/community relationships. I felt the latter had been taking place, so I began to assert my authority a little sooner than I would have normally done. Thus, step one is to plant the seeds of self-worth by privately, politely and quietly confronting them with what they have done wrong and patiently ask them either to stop or go back and undo something they have done. Of course I don't expect them to do it. That is not why I am telling them. I'm aware that in their minds they have no reason to obey; yet I also know that I am planting something deep inside their mind and hearts. I know I don't need to pay much attention to their outward rebellion or laughing at my "ridiculous" commands. I know I don't have to take it personal when they talk back or curse at me. I just know, for their own good, I can't let them get away with it. Why? Because, nobody feels good about himself or herself when they are unkind and disrespectful to parents, friends, or other people they really have no reason to disrespect. By correcting, clarifying, and confronting their "bad" behavior, I am awakening their sense of self-worth that was lost somewhere. I'm also aware that to rebuild a persons self-worth takes time. Thus, I don't expect them to obey me right away; it is just a matter of planting seeds of obedience, respect, cooperation and self-image. It is a seed that says, "I believe in you and know you are a better person than that". Then, step two is nurturing that seed into fruition. This is cultivated through being consistent, fair, non-petty, showing no favoritism, giving unconditional love and the ability to be flexible and reasonable when the situation calls for it. It helps them to separate what they do, from whom they are as human beings, worthy of dignity, acceptance and respect. If one can demonstrate these skills, it goes a long way in winning the respect and obedience of gang members and other defiant youth.

I have not, and do not always get it right. I have learned through making many mistakes and losing control of my temper, yelling and becoming visibly angry, etc. but the one thing we can have going for us, if we so choose, is the humility to admit when we are wrong and ask for forgiveness. I've never had a gang member reject my sincere apology or forgiveness. I have found them to be understanding and quick to forgive. As a matter of fact, I have found many times, this caused me to gain much more ground in our relationship than always doing things right. Not to say I made mistakes on purpose. But just that something happened in these kids when they could see that I was "real", that I too could fail in behavior, admit it and still be ok. This genuine humility can touch the deepest part of anybody's heart and spirit, helping them to grow in emotional maturity. I have had the hardest of the "hard core", come to me later and begin to open up and cry in the classroom, office, playground and even the jail cell. Once they saw how I dealt with my failure, they knew they could trust me and share their hearts with me. What gave them the courage to do this was all the times I demonstrated my forgiveness and unconditional love for them when they disrespected and mistreated me before.

I have seen this work over and over again when it comes to working with gang members and causing them to begin to change their behavior and attitudes. Someone has to demonstrate a new or different way of "seeing" things for them. Otherwise, why should they change? Why should they conform to what they hear everybody saying, but not watching anybody do? The question one must ask yourself in working with gang members is what do you really believe about them? What prejudices do you have that may have formed your opinions that are coming through loud and clear to them by your actions, not by what you say? Do you really believe that they can change and do you really count their worth as human beings on the same level as you count you're own or those in society who are "successful"? Do you just feel sorry for them and act concerned, but at a deeper level you feel they are inferior and could never really "make it"? If you find that you do feel like this, or in some other similar ways in your heart, there is no need to be afraid to admit it, or to beat yourself up. Just recognize it and realize that maybe working with these types of kids is not for you, or change your view of them, or both. One of the main causes of many of the problems and trouble that gang members get into is a result of policeman, principals of schools, public officials, and teachers having a wrong attitude, which flows out of a negative paradigm. We don't like to admit it, but our action under pressure only proves the reality of our lack of understanding and tolerance that we seem to have for other kinds of kids.

Sometimes the focus, when working with gang members, should not be on what wrong they did or are doing, but rather, why they did it or are doing it? On the other hand, another way of saying it is: "who provoked the negative behavior?" It is easy to provoke negative behavior from these kinds of kids. And it is a fact, that some, who work with these kids or have to deal with them on a consistent basis, enjoy provoking them into negative behavior that allows them to impose consequences, seemingly with justification. I have personally witnessed this, especially when I worked in the prison system as a correctional officer and in juvenile hall as a teachers aide.

Maybe those in authority, who are provoking kids into negative behavior, perhaps subconsciously, perhaps not, want to prove their assumptions that these are bad kids who can't change or be "saved". This gives them a reason to take the low and easy road to treat gang members with contempt and a self-righteous intolerance. This lazy minded way is found all too often among those who have to deal with gang members on a daily or at least fairly consistent basis. At times it is a lack of ability to emotionally and mentally deal with the attitudes of these kids. But other times it is a lack of willingness, on the part of the teacher or others in authority, to do the inner work of personal growth necessary, which prevents gang members from receiving the type of care, flexibility, kindness, patience, tolerance, and benefit of the doubt given to other "normal" kids.

If gang members are different from other kids, it is usually due to the environment they've had to endure that can include a lot of influences detrimental to their personal self-worth and identity. An emotional, psychological, and sometimes physically challenging circumstance many other kids do not have to experience. Yet, regardless of these things, I must always remember that they are human beings, before they are gang members, and thus, they are in no way inferior, have tremendous potential and sometimes need a different kind of help to uncover it.

We should not assume that a student's constant misbehavior means that they have no interest in learning to value education. Defiance or disobedience does not always mean that a student is unwilling or unable to cooperate."Clowning", does not only show an outward expression of a need for attention, but can also be a hint of hidden leadership ability that somehow was buried within. Most of the time, defiance and disobedience are clues to deeper issues that oftentimes can be effectively addressed by someone who simply believes in them, reaches out to them and validates their personal worth, something that they may not be receiving at home. Thus, we must learn to value relationships, more than wanting to be right. This takes humility. Too many teachers win the argument, but lose the relationship by constantly resorting to fronting off kids to show off their authority.

Humility is best defined as *power under control.* To illustrate this definition, picture a Great Dane lying down and doing nothing to a baby kitten that is pawing at him, hissing, and harassing him. This is power under control. With one swipe of his paw, a loud bark, or a quick bite, this dog could easily destroy and rid himself of this pesky cat. Yet, for some reason, he chooses not to, and instead chooses to exercise humility. Knowing when to exert your authority, or power, and when not to, is vital to winning over problem students.

While teaching is very rewarding, at the same time it can be very humbling, especially when you encounter uncooperative students on a daily basis. However, with problem students we face our finest, as well as our "forming" hour, if we practice the principle of humility. Through problems we discover our strengths and weaknesses. We learn how to confront adversity, and overcome it. Problem students provide us the opportunity to examine and evaluate ourselves at the end of the day, and realize that to become an effective teacher requires much more than mastering knowledge of a certain subject. It also reminds us that our education did not end with receiving a diploma, but rather was the beginning of our professional education in personal growth. Among other things, we can learn to master the arts of communication, building relationships, and inspiring motivation, all in a culturally diverse classroom. This may seem unrealistic, or idealistic, for the common classroom teacher. However, I suggest it requires this much and more to be an effective educator in many classrooms around the nation, that are overcrowded, culturally diverse and also consist of students with a variety of personal challenges they bring to school daily. Following this simple suggestion, of not "fronting off" problem students can go a long way in assisting the teacher in developing their classroom into an environment of learning and productive student participation.

Principle 2 – Honesty

Some people will not tolerate such emotional honesty in communication. They would rather defend their dishonesty on the grounds that it might hurt others. Therefore, having rationalized their phoniness into nobility, they settle for superficial relationships.
–Author Unknown

The double standard usually occurs when a teacher crosses the line verbally or physically but penalizes the student when they do the normal thing most kids do in this situation – retaliate in kind. I have personally witnessed this many times when the teacher initiated a sarcastic comment that started off "in fun", the student shot back an equally "fun" remark, to which the teacher, not only responded to, but took the sarcasm to another level, to which the student, not knowing how, where or when to quit, took it too far and ended up in the vice principals office for being disrespectful to the teacher, or something to that affect. However, the question is - who is going to hold the teacher accountable for their inappropriate behavior? The answer is, the teacher is really the only one that can hold themselves accountable, which will take the personal integrity of honesty, a virtue that can, in a short period of time, give a teacher much credibility that creates productivity in their students. Without the teacher holding themselves accountable for their part in the "drama", the student is left to defend themselves and tell their side of the story that "the teacher started it" and said this and that too, etc., but this all too often falls on the deaf ears of school administrators and little to nothing is done to the teacher, while the student can end up with any number of consequences; from after school detention to suspension, depending on the teacher, the vice principal and past history of the student. This causes a lot of resentment for the teacher and now the battle is “on”.

I remember witnessing this almost daily when I worked as a teacher’s aide in a juvenile hall facility. Some of the teacher’s and juvenile hall employees delighted in using this double standard as a means of provoking kids in trouble and in some cases causing kids to forfeit their release time and extending their stay because the kid would react to the teachers provoking of anger and inappropriate language and/or behavior. Some would even challenge the youth and tell them they would not make it through the day without getting in trouble so they could penalize them by sending them back to their cell or take away their recreation time or even worse, reporting them to their probation officer, who would then not release them on their previous release date and make them stay longer. The teachers would then proceed to harass and provoke the kid throughout the day to see if they could “win” the challenge, which they often did. Unfortunately some teachers, and others in positions of authority, are aware there’s a double standard and that they can get away with physically, emotionally or verbally abusing a youth without being accountable for their wrong behavior.

This issue of the “double standard” is important for a number of reasons, especially when dealing with at-risk youth involved in or on the fringes of being involved in a gang. What is often at the root of their cynicism for rules and defiance towards teachers is a rebellion against authority based on injustices or abuses they have experienced in their early years of development. They may have experienced this in a variety of settings, but it is most often experienced in their own homes as children that instinctively know it is wrong but may not know how to deal with it or articulate it at the moment it is happening. For example, they hear one or both of their parents cursing, but then get slapped across the mouth when they say the same words. They see one or both of their parents smoking and drinking but then get punished, sometimes in a severe manner, for doing the same things. They watch their parents lie about being sick and staying home from work, but then get punished for ditching school. They know that one or both of their parents are gang members, but then get their butt's kicked for hanging out with neighborhood gang kids. All of these examples imply a double standard that most kids don't understand, but grow to resent the fact that parents and/or those in authority play by a "different" set of rules than the one's they hold their kids to. In other words, they hold their kids to a standard higher than the one they themselves are willing to keep and thus, many gang members already have a negative attitude towards authority figures and have no respect for "rules" that apply in only one direction.

I understand that parents mean well in trying to hold their children to a higher moral standard than the one they live by (like when our parents used to make us go to church, but never went with us, etc.), and certainly there are times when it is a matter of age when parents stop punishing their kids for mimicking their habits such as smoking or drinking, cursing, etc. Nevertheless, in general, the double standard produces a justified cynicism for obedience to rules, and has for a long time become one of the main challenges teachers in the classroom face on a daily basis. Thus, how should a teacher deal with this cynicism for rules and defiance to their authority in the classroom? I suggest that one strong response is that of personal honesty, especially if the inappropriate behavior of their students was teacher initiated. My experience has been that personal honesty goes a long way in bringing children/students into a willing submission to classroom rules of behavior.

At the teen center that I mentioned in an earlier chapter, we had rules posted on the wall that all youth were expected to obey. The problem was that I had to get the staff to obey them before we could expect the kids to obey them (we eventually ended up re-writing the rules as there were too many and they were unrealistic for a teen center environment). It is a matter of modeling the appropriate behavior that we expect from those following us or under our supervision. More than once I remember losing my temper and angrily shouting at a gang member at the teen center that was disobeying the rules (AGAIN!) and/or a direct order from me or one of the staff members. Thus, they reacted in kind by yelling back at me and getting in my face, which was a violation of the rule to obey staff members and respect the staff and other members at all times. Yet, there I was breaking the rule of showing disrespect for a member of the teen center by yelling at them first. In other words, I initiated the anger and yelling. Now, I was the director, not only a staff member, and it would have been very easy for me to get my way, use my position of authority and "win" the confrontation without ever being held accountable for my wrong behavior. However, knowing that everyone, staff and teen center members, were watching me, and that I could not let the kid get away with their defiant behavior with no consequences (which would send a loud message to the other kids), and more importantly that I had initiated the yelling at me by yelling at them first, I had to decide what to do. I decided to be honest with myself and I apologized to the kid for yelling at him and asked him to forgive me. Of course this completely disarmed him, he accepted my apology and I proceeded to explain to him why I could not allow him to do what he was doing and we resolved the problem.

I am not suggesting by this one example that a teacher can always respond this way, or that personal honesty will always work to resolve the immediate problem at hand, but then again, I have seen it work so often that I know it does work and is a powerful way of helping rebellious kids as they witness a model of one standard of obedience to rules that applies especially to those who create and enforce the rules and don't expect kids to live a different standard than their own.

PRINCIPLE 3 – COMMUNICATION

Talking is like playing on the harp; there is as much in laying the hands on the strings to stop their vibration as in twanging them to bring out their music.
–Oliver Wendell Holmes

Oftentimes teachers and school administrators are unaware that their instructions and explanations go right over the heads of many of their students because of their choice of words. I've accompanied many students to meetings with a teacher or the vice-principal (as their advocate) and sitting there with the student listening to what they were being told. One particular time as the vice-principal was trying to convey to the student that if they didn't want to be considered a gang member, they should not be associated in any way with gang members, she said, *"If it walks like a duck, talks like a duck, and acts like a duck, then it probably is a duck"*. After we left the office I asked, "Did you understand what the V.P. was saying to you?" to which the student replied, "No". This was not a matter of whether or not the student could understand or speak English, but simply a matter of the choice of words used and being unaware of not being understood. I can hear some teachers saying, "Well I'm not going to come down to their level of speech, they are going to have to come up to mine", well OK, but in the meantime, they still don't understand. This is a dilemma because students should improve their vocabulary. Yet, what would it hurt us to explain things in a couple of ways in order to make sure we are teaching and not just talking?

As teachers we are primarily communicators and one of the key principles for quality communication is to understand your audience. To know who you are speaking to and at what level to share your knowledge, information or message so that it penetrates in a lasting and effective way. Vocabulary is a matter of who I am speaking to. One set of words for one audience and another set of words for another. I speak one way around my family and friends, another around professionals and still another around teens. The issue is not simply talking and being heard by the listeners, but rather using my words to connect with my audience and engaging their heart and mind to at least understand, if not also to agree, with the message or teaching.

The other important key in communication is our ability to listen empathetically, or to practice "empathic listening" as it is called. Of course this is not always practical in the daily setting of a classroom. However, whenever possible, I suggest that if a teacher, who is dealing with a difficult student that is constantly disrupting the class, could make time for listening, (a powerful form of communication) the student will many times reciprocate and listen when the teacher is teaching. This attentiveness, coupled with the teacher's appropriate vocabulary will make for a productive classroom environment. I am not suggesting that a teacher should not incorporate "new words" into the instruction so as to help student's increase and improve their vocabulary. I am suggesting that more value be given to whether or not true communication is taking place between the instructor and the students. One measure of true communication is the ability of the instructor to communicate knowledge and important information in terms that the student understands. After all, effective teaching is really not a matter of what the teacher knows, but how much the students know what the teacher knows.

In his classic book, "Reforming Education", a book that addresses the question of what can be done to improve American Education, Mortimer J. Adler states;

> *"The teacher must put himself sympathetically in the position of a learner, who is less advanced than himself, less advanced in skill and in knowledge or understanding. From that vantage point, he must reenact – or stimulate – for the learner the activities he himself engaged in to achieve his present state of mind...Genuine teaching, in sharp distinction from indoctrination, always consists in activities on the part of teachers that cooperate with activities performed by the minds of students engaged in discovery."*

I suggest this will not happen without a careful choice of vocabulary by the teacher, inquiry as to whether or not students understand, and using different ways and/or methods of explaining the lesson to be learned. In addition, the teacher must work to create a safe environment for ignorance. This means that the teacher will not, nor will allow other students to, laugh at and/or belittle students who have the courage to ask clarifying questions, whose answers might seem obvious to the teacher or others in the class. The wise and effective teacher understands that the more questions their students ask, the better they will learn if their vocabulary is effectively communicating in the classroom.

Principle 4 - Tolerance

"In the practice of tolerance,
one's enemy is the best teacher."
- Fourteenth Dalai Lama

One of the great qualities of all the world's most influential religious teachers such as; Buddha, the Prophet Mohamed, Confucius and Jesus Christ, is their demonstration of patience and understanding for the ignorance of their followers as they endeavored to take them to deeper levels of knowledge, wisdom and spiritual insight. For example, there are many examples of the disciples of Christ asking for an explanation and greater understanding of the sometimes very unorthodox teaching of Jesus. What patience and understanding he exemplified for us teachers as he walked the disciples through their ignorance and into the deeper knowledge of eternal truths. The tolerance and understanding, skill and simplicity with which he dealt with their ignorance serves as a good model for any would be teacher, aspiring to reach the not so easy to teach.

Ignorant is what we all are when it comes to a new area of knowledge, and the gulf between knowledge and ignorance can be deep and wide depending on a number of different factors such as age, culture, background, language, emotional health, and motivation to learn, just to name a few. The wise teacher is aware and empathetic to all these factors and assumes nothing about those they are about to teach a new, or different level of a particular subject. They keep in mind that they were also once ignorant of many things and it was because of someone who had the patience and tolerance for their ignorance that allowed them to grow and gain the knowledge and expertise they now possess. This understanding and attitude helps students to learn and not be afraid to show their ignorance to a teacher who they feel safe with because they are assured, encouraged, and understood by the "master teacher". Thus, tolerance for ignorance is an essential quality teacher's need.

The effective teacher knows that expertise or knowledge of the subject matter is not enough, but must be coupled with understanding of their students in order to effectively communicate and cause the transfer of knowledge from the learned to the ignorant. The ability to take what is difficult and make it simple, or at least seem simple, is the teacher's task.

"The ability to simplify means to eliminate the unnecessary so that the necessary may speak."
- Hans Hofmann

A teacher is one who clarifies, sheds light on a new path, and while this is not always easy, it goes a long way in the classroom where students are dependent on the teacher for growing in knowledge. However, if the teacher lacks this quality of tolerance and patience with the ignorant, it can make for a frustrating time for both the teacher and students. I'll never forget an incident that took place in my seventh grade math class, which was loaded with the "lower track" students in regards to our capacity in math problem solving. One day the teacher was frustrated because we just weren't "getting it" and he decided to pick on one of the students by asking him in front of the whole class what the "obvious" answer was to the problem he was showing us on the chalk board. I remember sitting there as the teacher continued to ask my friend for the answer and berating him each time he answered incorrectly, to which we all laughed for each wrong answer and to which the teacher grew angrier and angrier. *"Come on Stephen, this is one you can get right"* I remember saying to myself as we could all see the anger building up in the teacher's face. He finally called my friend up to the front of the class to embarrass him even more and finally grew so angry that he slapped him across the head (back then corporal punishment had not yet been outlawed) because he couldn't answer what was a seemingly easy problem to solve that he had been explaining for most of the time in the class. The class suddenly grew silent and I will never forget the look of embarrassment, humiliation and loss of dignity on Stephen's face that day due to the teachers' lack of tolerance for ignorance. It wasn't that my friend knew the answer and was just trying to give the teacher a bad time or "front him off" to make the class laugh at the teacher. He really did not know the answer, but worse yet; he was really trying to figure it out as we all laughed and the teacher got angry.

This might seem like an extreme example, and of course today teachers are not allowed to touch kids, let alone slap their heads! But, the point is the student in the above scenario did not learn, grow or advance in knowledge that day and I can't help but wonder how often this occurs in the classroom, particularly with "at-risk" youth, where the teacher has little tolerance for student's who can't "keep up" and either doesn't know how or doesn't want to go the extra mile to re-explain in different terms, exercise patience or try to understand what is holding back a student or the class from growing in their learning of the subject matter at hand. Don't get me wrong here; I am not suggesting that a teacher put up with consistent defiance and lack of cooperation from unmotivated students in their classes. I have been on both sides of that equation and understand quite well that a defiant, unmotivated student is sometimes beyond the patience and tolerance I am talking about here. Nevertheless, isn't it also that a teacher needs to acknowledge their lack of tolerance for ignorance, and I suggest that one way to counter this is by responding to ignorance with understanding first and then seek to be understood by the student. Dr. Stephen Covey calls this one of the *7 Habits of Highly Effective People*; "seek first to understand", and I believe if teachers practice this principle with students who are having difficulty grasping the knowledge in a particular subject, it will eventually produce the transfer of knowledge needed. There is something very liberating to the soul when it feels "understood". Nevertheless, there is equally something very defeating when the soul feels miss-understood:

> *"The author of this study also refers to the feeling of scholastic inadequacy which characterizes Mexican American students, illustrating this reaction by quoting a University graduate who made the following comment about drop outs: "It was very hard for Mexican students...the teachers would run them down for being so dumb all the time. Most of them just got sick of it and dropped out of school."*

The above quote was taken from a study that was published in 1960, *Mexican American Youth: forgotten youth at the crossroads, by Celia S. Hunter of Hunter College (Random House).* It is very interesting to read this study and realize that not much has changed in the public schools since that time. But for our purposes here, the above quote re-enforces my suggestion on the principle of tolerance for ignorance, especially when it is understood that many Hispanic/Latino student gang members are coming into the situation with cultural, environmental and emotional handicaps that many other students are not dealing with and any hint by the teacher that gives these students the perception of inferiority, is a sure catalyst for the ongoing statistical nightmare of the Latino student drop out rate. On a positive note regarding this, the study also showed the positive influence school personnel can have on students; *"...the teacher probably occupies a strategic position for influencing Mexican American upward mobility. One gains insight into the potential importance of this position when talking with Mexican Americans who have been occupationally successful. Careful questioning reveals that there is almost always an individual, often a teacher or principal, whom such mobile persons credit for their accomplishments. For example, a Mexican American college graduate described his school history; "I was discouraged about even going to elementary school until I reached the fifth grade...I had been kicked out of four schools already as a problem child. In the fifth grade, at California Street School, the principal, without asking any questions as to why I had transferred, asked if I wanted to be a safety monitor...from then on I became interested in school in spite of the fact that I was afraid the other boys would razz me for being a school stooge. Another Mexican American, a student at the University at California, testified: "As long as I live I will never forget a sixth grade teacher I had...her encouragement made me want to make something of myself. She planted the seeds of college in my head...words of encouragement and acceptance meant a great deal to me."*

One final aspect of the tolerance for ignorance principle is awareness of the expectation of Latino parents. Today, as it was during the time of the above referred to study, many parents of Latino students are primarily Spanish speaking and have had a minimal amount of formal education, or have had the minimal education of going through, or part way through, high school. These parents assume that teachers are aware of their situation, understand why they have not learned English and therefore speak Spanish to their children, which they realize puts them at a disadvantage in the American, English speaking classroom. However, they expect that the "schools' job, i.e. principals and teachers' job, is to deal with this obvious and understandable disadvantage. This is one reason why many of these parents do not participate in school functions because they don't see that as their role or their place. They expect the school to deal with all aspects of their child's education and their role is to deal with the domestic aspects of life. This is often mistaken for a lack of caring about the education of their children, but nothing could be further from the truth. In the past, when schools decided to deal with the dual language issue by not allowing Hispanic/Latino students to speak Spanish in school period (or at least in the classroom), parents did not make too much of a fuss over this because, again, that was not their place and they were speaking Spanish and inculcating their children with their cultural values at home anyway. Today of course we have the bi-lingual classroom, but the point is that as far as parents are concerned, with or without bi-lingual classrooms, they expect the school to educate their children successfully. They expect that the professional educators are tolerant of the situation and will make every effort to equalize, or "level the playing field". They do not expect racism, prejudice or the intolerance that I am addressing here, from "los professores" (The teachers). In our culture, teachers and school principals are held in very high esteem and there is an assumed professionalism on the part of the parents that their "mijo and mija" are being given nothing but the best educational and school campus experience possible. Unfortunately, this naïve expectation is quickly dispelled all too often as parents begin to learn that little "Juan" is causing problems and not learning or cooperating or achieving like he should. The first reaction of the Latino parent is; "What's wrong with the school or teacher?" As I have been careful to point out in this book, in my opinion, the parent has the major role in assuring the future success of their child(ren). However, second to the parent is the teacher and my passion is to encourage the teachers role as an inspiration to Latino gang-bangers in the classroom, and exercising or developing tolerance for ignorance is one way of doing so.

Principle 5 - Poise

"Self command is the main elegance"

- Ralph Waldo Emerson

One of the greatest lessons I learned while serving as a correctional officer in two prisons was not to take myself too seriously or I would become the target of the inmates' daily game of seeing whose "buttons" they could push to cause an officer to lose emotional control, or their "professional poise" in one way or another. It became a game, a bet, to see how long it would take to cause the officer to explode with anger. The inmates very rarely meant much of what they said, and did not care that much about the stuff they did, it was all about pushing buttons and just good entertainment for people in their daily situation. Working in this type of environment is like a daily "psychological war" game and it can cause you a lot of frustration and anger. It begins to cause you to come to work with a vendetta to get back at the person, or people for exploiting your emotions like this on a regular basis.

One crude, but poignant example of this is the lesson all correctional officers learn about answering their house floor phone and that is that you never answer that phone without looking at the receiver first! Why?, because one of the "games" inmates like to play is with the phone receiver. It rings all day and night as officers communicate back and forth from different areas of the prison and they pick up the phone quickly and put it to their ear and talk, etc. However, what inmates like to do from time to time for a laugh, is to sneak and smear human excrement on the receiver and when the office picks up the phone without looking at it first and puts it to their ear, well you can imagine the rest. I witnessed this happening to a female officer one day that the inmates did not particularly care for and what a scene that was! To this day I still never answer any phone without looking at it first! Thus, in general it follows that if those of us in leadership or positions of authority, working in a high risk environment begin to take ourselves too seriously, it can cause us to become a target to those who love to provoke you out of your comfort zone.

My staff and I would fight this psychological war everyday at the teen center. The kids loved to do this "button pushing", as I call it, as a kind of soft way of rebelling or defying authority from a place where the provoker is relatively on safe ground since he or she is really not doing anything too serious other than just playing with your mind too see how far they can go and learn what makes you tick and where your anger buttons are, etc. And believe me, most of the time, it is a planned event and the "innocent" by-standers are usually part of the plot and have talked the one provoker into the act that they all believe will get the desired result of anger that they can all laugh at later. After dealing with this in the prisons, school campuses and at the teen center, I learned it doesn't hurt to lighten up, loosen up and be able to laugh at yourself once in awhile and not be so serious 100% of the time even though you might be in a tough daily environment like a teen center working with at-risk youth or a classroom with student gang members who love to push your buttons.

I remember back in junior high school a few of my friends and I decided to give a "pay back" to our teacher as she always seemed to be "picking" on one of us (of course the truth is we were always disrupting the class). On this particular day, I was chosen to be the "provoker" by placing a thumb tack on the stool she always sat on when she was addressing the class. The excitement and anticipation for those of us in "the know" was just too much fun and things got out of hand when the moment came and she sat on her stool only to jump right back out of it with an awkwardness and disfigured face that none of us could maintain our poise and were somehow implicated as having something to do with it. I am sure you get "the point" (pun intended) by this story and what I am discussing here, that when we take ourselves too seriously and don't seem to possess the ability to have a little levity in our learning environment (which this teacher clearly did not have) sometimes others will take it into their own hands to break the monotonous monotone of seriousness.

One thing about us "Latinos/Chicanos" is that we love to "cap" (slang for making fun of) and play "practical jokes" and if a teacher has a room full of us she can expect that a lot of capping and practical jokes will take place. If she can learn to "take it", or better yet, learn how to "cap" back, without crossing the line, it goes a long way with Latino students in developing rapport, respect and receptiveness of instruction. The wise thing to do when one finds themselves the victim of "capping" is to respond with poise and laughter, or at least a smile (not in the case of the thumb tack incident of course, that went way beyond capping), which will signal to the one capping (and everyone else watching) that you can "take it". Believe it or not, with most Latino youths, this goes a long way in building rapport and earning their respect, especially if you are quick witted and know how to "come back" in a way that makes the others go, "ooohhhhhh" and make the person who capped on you laugh while their face turns red!

Having "poise" or practicing the principle of poise was not something we learned in "teachers' school". However, as we know, our education did not end when we graduated but really began the day we entered the real world of the daily classroom and developing poise is a skill we need and can still acquire. Thus, I suggest that understanding and learning to develop our poise will help us encounter and overcome some of the daily battles we will most likely encounter in working with "at-risk" or defiant and disobedient youth.

The word poise is defined as; *a counterweight, regulating power, balance, equilibrium, self-possession and composure.* It is a kind of inner tranquility, that some have suggested is one of the best ways to manifest one's true power and authority or command of the situation. This is important to understand because while the classroom is ideally a place of learning, it is often a place of a subtle and sometimes not so subtle battle for control and power. And thus, the teacher needs a strategy that will produce a win for them and a win for the students. Thinking "win-win", as Dr. Covey suggests, is vital on the "psychological battlefield" because if all we concern ourselves with is winning for ourselves, we can miss the other opportunity that exists which is the conversion of our "competition" while at the same time establishing our control and power in the classroom. How is this done? One way is through the exercising of our poise as a "counterweight" or balance to the disruptive, rude and defiant behavior meant to intimidate us and render us powerless as an authority figure in our own domain. As I stated, this is a battle that must be won by the teacher, yet, there is more to winning than just squelching and defeating your competition, which is within the power of the teacher to do and usually the instinctive reaction of power in the classroom. I suggest that a choice to respond with tranquility and poise during times of being the subject of laughter is a powerful demonstration of control and power that can not only give others a sense of security and peacefulness, but also serve to win over their hearts as they witness a better way of handling disrespect, discourteousness and discomfort.

"Remember that there is always a limit to
self-indulgence, but none to self-restraint."
–Mahatma Gandhi

By way of illustration, I'll share one of the most fearful experiences I had as a correctional officer (CO). I was new on the job and little did I know it was my time to be tested in the fire by the inmates, and perhaps my fellow officers. In order to be a "bull" (affectionate name for a CO given by the inmates) one goes through intensive training to prepare you to live, work and operate within "the world" of the inmates. It is definitely a "society within a society" as anybody who has been in or worked in a prison on a regular basis knows. At the time this incident took place I had the central quad supervision duty, which was essentially supervising the traffic of inmates leaving their particular locked, fenced and gun tower guarded housing section, otherwise known as a "quad", into a different part of the prison for various reasons such as going to work, a class, or a church service and the like. One of our duties was that if there was ever commotion or action in other parts of the prison we were to react and get there as soon as possible to help in what was usually an emergency type of situation. We wore "beepers" and when an officer set it off, we all knew there was trouble and would be directed to the place where the incident was taking place. In this particular instance, I was notified to go to quad "D", building # 1. In each quad there were four buildings each with three floors and one hundred cells per floor. One officer was assigned to each floor, or one hundred inmates, and from 9 pm to 12 am there was a fourth officer in the building known as a rover. As you can imagine, a floor officer can never leave his floor supervision duties for the entire time he is on his shift, except for the most extreme situations, like when a beeper goes off, and all available officers in the immediate area are supposed to respond because this means an officer is calling for immediate help.

So here is what happened; my beeper went off and I ran from the central quad area into quad "D' and building # 1. To my surprise when I came flying through the door, there was no one there except a crowd of inmates. I looked around and they began to surround me and in my mind I was thinking, "where the heck is everybody!!!". At that point a big, tall inmate began to talk "smack" to me and challenge me and said he was going to find out what I was made of, etc. To be honest, he would have found out what I "was made of", because he probably would have torn me apart. Although I'd like to think I could have handled my own, he was just too big and too strong for me and I knew it. But, because I did have a lot of "street" experience of fighting in these kinds of situations I knew that I had to keep my poise. I did not understand it in those terms, but I just knew I could not panic and get crazy by moving forward in slugging and kicking, nor could I show any signs of backing down or fear. It was clearly a losing situation for me as I stood there alone surrounded by Black, White and Latino inmates on their turf all the while wondering why no one else was showing up. I did not know it at the time, but this was my "initiation" or "hazing", if you will, into the prison fraternity and I will never know if the other officers were in on it or not, but all I know is that this whole scene went down and not one other officer ever showed up in this "beeper" emergency situation. All of a sudden, as the inmate was removing his shirt and I took my stance to defend myself, another inmate spoke up and said, "OK, that's enough" and the guy put his shirt back on, turned around and walked away. I stood there looking up at this other inmate, who was obviously the "shot caller", stunned. Then he turned around and left and so did everybody else, including me. What is my point? It was my poise that saved me that day because as I later found out from an inmate, that whole scene was about finding out if I had any "heart". He said I had passed simply because I had not backed down. As I said, that was a very scary experience, but I said all that to say this, exercising the principle of poise, rather than emotional reaction, under pressure can be very effective in handling a tough situation. In dealing with gang members in the classroom, hopefully a teacher will not have to be in such a tense situation. However the fact is that sometimes student gang members will try to intimidate a teacher out of their control of the student and/or classroom, which is the subject of the next section and principle.

PRINCIPLE 6 – MEEKNESS

Meekness is not weakness, but rather controlled strength. It is the opposite of pride.

Fear and intimidation can be a powerful tool in the hand of a student gang member. It is something the teacher must do their best never to give into. If a student is using the tactic of intimidation on the teacher and perceives that the teacher is afraid, it will be considered a sign of weakness and it can result in a tough battle to earn the upper hand of respect and control of the classroom. As in the example of my encounter with the inmate, if I had revealed weakness, that news would have traveled through the prison "grapevine" quickly and I would have had a much harder time earning respect and trying to do my job of controlling and holding inmates accountable to the "rules" as the job constantly calls for. This of course is the objective of intimidation and fear, but in a classroom situation the teacher can often overcome this through the power of meekness. This may at first seem like a response of weakness in itself and certainly there are times when a teacher will have to assert themselves in a forceful and firm manner in order to take control or use fear and intimidation themselves when the situation calls for it. But in general, meekness can be a better way of winning the war over the long haul, even though one may seemingly lose the current battle. I am not suggesting that the teacher in an intimidating situation won't feel the emotion of fear or even show that they are somewhat afraid, as I did in facing down the inmate. But this display of outward emotion does not mean we are not willing to confront the situation and stay in the battle for control, respect and compliance of the disruptive student to the same standards of conduct and productivity expected of everyone else. For example, if a student threatens or physically gets in the face of the teacher, and is obviously bigger and stronger or believed to be capable of causing harm, at that moment, a teacher may feel scared, look scared and in fact be intimidated and back down in that moment. However, what let's the student know that they have only won one battle and that the war itself is not over, is when the teacher will continue to enforce what was expected. Believe me, if a teacher can manage this, it will be a major deposit in the hearts of the other students and gain her a lot of respect and cooperation from the others, and some will even come to her defense in the moment or later on. In other words we are showing the student(s) gang member that we will not be intimidated or fearful to hold them accountable, and yet at the same time take the higher road of doing our jobs and still treat them with the dignity, respect and unconditional love that we ourselves would want in return. We will not allow them to dictate to us, and make us make them our "enemy" for that would be playing right into their hand. We are beyond that. We will not be bullied into always kicking them out of class and sending them to the vice principals office, though that may be what they deserve, we are in control and may choose not to give them what they deserve! We are not afraid to forgive, understand, turn the other cheek and demonstrate "power under control", which is the true definition of "meekness".

Choosing to respond with the principle of meekness is not a sign of "weakness", but rather it is a sign of true power in the stronger (whether it be physically, intellectually, authoritatively or morally) position, choosing not to exercise our power at the moment for their sakes. I can not count all the times I have chosen this response in situations where I clearly had the upper hand when being challenged physically, mentally or emotionally by students, gang members and my own children as a father disciplining my children. In the case of my children, they appeal to and attack my emotions by saying they "hate" me and that I am "mean" and don't understand them and not cool like so and so's parents that allow them to do what I am not allowing them to do, etc. I am sure all parents know what I am talking about. To this day my kid's remind me of this once in a while and laughingly tell me; "Hey dad, remember when we used to tell you we "hated" you because you we're not letting us get our way?" But what stuck with them was the response I always gave them when they said "I hate you", I would respond with, "Well you might hate me, but I love you".

Allow me to share one more story to illustrate the power of meekness in dealing with tough situations, especially when we are trying to win over our "enemies" so to speak.

A member of my church, who was a heavy duty drug user and had spent a lot of time in prison became a real problem that I had to confront. He and his brothers were well known for drug dealing and other violent activities. I built what I thought was a good relationship with this person and went out of my way many times for him in a variety of ways as his pastor. However, he would often go in and out of his violent tendencies, stopped attending church, and would go back to abusing drugs and alcohol, as is often the case in helping people dealing with these issues. At one point he began to make demands on me that I just could not accept. He then began to intimidate me with death threats and violence that he and his brothers would do against me, my wife and kids. Had I doubted his capability of such actions I might have blown it off. But I knew he and his brothers were very capable and I lost several nights of sleep over it as "tonight" always became the night he was going to carry out the threats. Some of you are probably wondering why I did not call the police, and maybe I should have, but having worked in the prison and understanding his mentality of "fingering" or "ratting" him out, I just did not think that was the right course of action to solve this real threat. Finally, one night after another threatening call, I was so fed up with his threats that I hung up and decided to take him by surprise and showed up at his house. One of his brothers answered the door and let me in. He (my "friend") was shocked to see me and I calmly began to tell him that this had to end. He immediately starting cursing at me and then slapped me across the face. Now, in my mind I clearly had the upper hand physically and by the fact that he was high on whatever and I wasn't. However, when his brother saw my non-reaction of turning the other cheek, he immediately stepped in and pulled him away from me and told me to leave, which I did but not before I made it clear that I was not going to tolerate this any longer (I didn't know what I was going to do, but I said it anyway). The following day, this guy felt so bad about hitting me and just the fact that I did not retaliate, he came to the church and literally fell on his knees and crying asked me to forgive him, which I did and the problem never surfaced again and his loyalty to our relationship was then stronger for it.

This is obviously a very extreme example and to be sure, I certainly would never recommend to anybody to take the course of action I did, but I only share it to drive home the point of the power of the principle of meekness and forgiveness to someone opposing you. I am sure there are teachers, principals, policemen, pastors and parents reading this, who could share similar stories about the power of demonstrating meekness as one response to fear and intimidation, and while it may not always work, or may not always be what we are able to decide to do, it does work as a matter of principle over time. Thus, sometimes we have to fight fire with fire, and sometimes we have to fight fire with water, but we never want to fight fire with gasoline, which is too often the case when teachers and students clash in the classroom and things only get worse for all concerned when anger rules as the weapon of choice. The balance between meekness and weakness is that on the one hand I choose to keep my power under control, but on the other hand I refuse to accept being disrespected and will not give in to intimidation in my home, area, school or classroom.

Principle 7 – Priorities

Taking first things first often reduces the most complex human problem to a manageable proportion
– Dwight D. Eisenhower

Of the seven issues I have discussed here, this is one of the most common and emotionally exhausting mistakes a teacher can fall into, and while student gang members can respect rules, they resent pettiness, recognize it readily, and usually react very negatively to it. In general I think most of us also resent pettiness when we encounter it in our daily lives. For example, I remember getting "swatted" with the paddle in junior high school for allowing my shirt tail to hang outside of my pants! Can you imagine such a rule in today's school environment? Was that really important? Did this rule really teach me something about character or improve my self-image? What was the underlying principle or concern that was going on with that? In other words, what was the root cause of the rule and could there not have been a better rule to develop whatever the school was trying to develop in its students. Wasn't that really a petty rule? Well you may agree or disagree, but it was enforced with consistency and rigor on mine and others behinds. The funny thing was that it was only my friends and others of our ethnicity that seemed to dress with that particular style, most others tucked there shirts in.

I realize that even today some schools do have a dress code, but this usually has to do with trying to keep the gang dress and colors off the school campus, or trying to keep enough clothes on girls to avoid too much attention from male students and faculty alike, and not just a matter of preference in style as in the case I am referring to "back in the day". I also remember that the girls vice-principal would stand in the hallway and pick out girls wearing skirts above the knee and would literally pull out a ruler and measure how high above the knee the skirt was right in front of everyone else!. If it exceeded the "legal length" (which was not very high), the girl would be sent home to change. Or how about the police officer who pulls you over at two o'clock in the morning for "rolling" through a stop sign (lovingly referred to as "the California roll", as one cop put it and I had hoped he was talking about sushi, but he wasn't) when there is nobody else in sight for miles and instead of warning you, actually writes you a ticket! I am sure many of you reading this could tell your own stories of frustrating "pettiness". In the case of the classroom, pettiness can be in the form of being penalized for arriving seconds after the tardy bell rings, not having a pencil or your book, or some other infraction of a whole bunch of rules the teacher has listed.

I realize that the examples I have given here may not seem "petty" to some, but the point is the fact that schools and teachers *can* be petty and I suggest this only leads to emotional and physical energy that could be better spent than trying to play "gotcha" because of all the rules in place that set students up for failure. Of course the question is, what defines pettiness, and lest I impose more of my opinions of what constitutes "pettiness", here is Webster's definition: *insignificant; trivial; narrow-minded; or mean."* Thus, however the teacher decides to define what rules are petty or not, I suggest the teacher make every effort to avoid falling into the daily "cat and mouse" game that pettiness invites and that some students love to play. This is a definite lose/lose situation and, as I stated, a waste of time and emotional energy. To avoid this emotional time trap, the teacher must decide what is important, what their priorities are, based on principle, rather than subjective "pet peeves" when it comes to classroom culture and the rules of conduct. The wise teacher develops his priorities and rules that can be legitimately defended even by the students themselves, and thus knows they are rules worth fighting for. Much like parents, we must choose our battles carefully, lest we be drawn into and "die on the wrong battlefield". We must know where we will draw the "line in the sand" and when that line is crossed we will take action for the long term good of the whole class and to demand the respect we have earned. This takes discussion, decisiveness and discernment all of which is gained through years of experience. A general rule of thumb is that too many rules, too many policies, and too much "zero tolerance" only begs for petty enforcement rather than discretion that allows for the solutions of student buy in, positive motivation and a transition to transforming cooperation.

One idea to avoid being petty, or being perceived as being petty, is when at all possible include the students in designing the class rules and the punishment for breaking "their" rules. Once the priorities, rules and consequences for both obeying the rules and breaking the rules are agreed upon, the teacher and/or students can "indoctrinate" the other classes the teacher has (in the junior and high school setting), letting them know that the rules were developed by their peers and the teacher. A focus group can potentially be formed that is represented by one student from each period/class. I know that this may not work or be possible in all circumstances, but it does work in some situations and it is understood that the rules and consequences are not in stone and can be reviewed and revised when necessary. By the way, this is a good way of teaching kids the basics of how our laws are made and ratified in civic life and the role of citizens in the process. Another tool for the teacher who has children of their own, is to ask them to evaluate the classroom rules or discuss with them situations they've come across and what they did about it. Youth have a keen sense and intuition of pettiness that we adults seem to lose the older we get. This does not mean that they are always right or that we have to follow their advice all the time, but sometimes they are right and following their advice can work for you.

There is no question that emotional energy is needed in the classroom and most teachers are "spent" or empty at the end of each day as they work through all the preparation of lessons, instruction and dealing with the daily drama from period to period, let alone the drama with other teachers, the administration, parents and possibly their own personal life. Thus, the last thing a teacher needs is to "spend" or waste their time on the "small" issues, rather than "investing" their time in the "larger" issues of educating children. If one is not careful to examine their assumptions and objectively evaluate their classroom culture, pettiness can rule the day and steal the joy, satisfaction and significance of teaching.

Bibliography

Berrios, Reynaldo. 2006. *Cholo Style – homies, homegirls & la raza.* Los Angeles: Reynaldo Berrios and Feral House

Curyk, Elsa. 2005. *The Hard Core Speak.* Victoria, BC, Canada: Trafford

Hayden, Tom. 2004, 2005. *Street Wars. New York: The New Press*

Hernandez, Arturo. 1998. *Peace in the Streets – Breaking the Cycle of Gang Violence.* Washington DC: Child Welfare League of America

Klein, Malcolm, W. 1995. *The American Street Gang: its nature, prevalence and control.* New York: Oxford University Press

Klein, Malcolm, W., Maxson, Cheryl, L. 2006. *Street Gang Patterns and Policies.* New York: Oxford University Press

Knox, George, W. 2006. *An Introduction to Gangs.* Peotone: New Chicago School Press, Inc.

Moore, Joan, W. 1991. *Going Down to the Barrio – Homeboys and Homegirls in Change.* Philadelphia: Temple University Press

Rafael, Tony. 2007. *The Mexican Mafia.* New York: Encounter Books

Ramos, Richard, R. 2006: *Got Gangs? – Practical Guidelines for Parents/Teachers on a Mission for Gang Prevention/Intervention.* Denver: Outskirts Press

Schumacher, Michael, Kurz, Gwen, A. 2000. *The 8% Solution – Preventing Serious, Repeat Juvenile Crime.* Thousand Oaks: Sage Publications, Inc.

Spergel, Irving, A. 1995. *The Youth Gang Problem – A Community Approach.* New York: Oxford University Press

Vigil, James, Diego. 2002. *A Rainbow of Gangs – Street Culture in the Mega City.* Austin. University of Texas Press

References

www.gangprograms.com

The Phoenix Curriculum provides two separate program elements: 1) The in-school Gang Prevention Curriculum is designed for elementary, middle school and high school student

2) The supplemental Gang Intervention Curriculum provides elementary, middle, and high schools with classroom and counseling-based curricula, designed for the higher risk students, and targeting the highest risk factors

www.advanceproj.org

The Advancement Project Los Angeles, a non-profit policy and legal action organization working to solve public sector problems. See - Release of "A Call to Action: A Case for a Comprehensive Solution to LA's Gang Violence Epidemic"

www.safeyouth.org

National Youth Violence Resource Center - latest national statistics on gangs

http://www.ojjdp.ncjrs.gov/ojstatbb/nr2006/index.html

Juvenile Offenders and Victims Report 2006 - Juvenile Offenders and Victims: 2006 National Report draws on reliable data and relevant research to provide a comprehensive and insightful view of juvenile crime across the nation.

http://www.stedwards.edu/educ/eanes/ganghome.html

Best practices for Gang prevention and intervention: Answers the basic questions of why kids join gangs, what are gangs, how can schools and communities help prevent and intervene in gang involvement by youth and provides links to other resources

www.focusas.com/Gangs.html

Provides awareness, prevention, education and great resources and links

www.gripe4rkids.org

Bringing the Community together to prevent Gangs and Crime. Provides good education and links

www.stedwards.edu/edu/eanes/ganghome.html

A study in best practices for gang prevention / intervention

www.gangwar.com

Information, blogs, education, research and resources for gang prevention / intervention

www.fastennetwork.org/Display.asp?Page=gangstats

Great resource for gang crime statistics in the U.S.

www.streetgangs.com

A list of organizations that reach out to and work with youth gang members

www.helpinggangyouth.org

Very good resource for books, research information, community strategic planning and variety of links on gangs

www.gottfredson.com/gang.htm

Findings from surveys of school-based gang prevention – intervention programs

www.iir.com/nygc

Another good source for national gang statistics and demographics

www.jrsa.org/jjec/index.html

Juvenile Justice Evaluation Center working closely with the Office of Juvenile Justice Delinquency Prevention (OJJDP) to evaluate Juvenile Justice programs in the U.S.

www.nationalgangcenter.gov

Collaboration between the Office of Justice Programs (OJP), the Bureau of Justice (BJA) and OJJDP featuring the latest information about anti-gang programs and a wide range of links and resources

www.godsxgangsters.org

Ex-gang members reaching out to the community and raising up leaders to go back into gang neighborhoods using dance, rap, drama and technology

NOTES

NOTES